Playing for Time

Coming to Light, An Advent Progress

&

Green, Blue, Brown

Rodney Kleber

Jimson House
Northampton, Massachusetts

Printed in the United States of America
Prepared for publication by: Darlene Swanson • www.van-garde.com

ISBN: 978-0-578-73547-4 (paperback)
978-0-578-77859-4 (ebook)

Jimson House
jimsonhouse@gmail.com
Northampton, MA

For Diane

"The Case of the Mysterious Maiden" has appeared with *Negative Capability*, "Pinwheel" with *The Nation*, "Mary Among Us" with *Dappled Things*, "December Romance" with *The Society of Classical Poets*, "N" with *The Ottawa Arts Review*, "Caught" and "In Place" with *The Deronda Review*, and "The House Sparrow" with *Slant*.

Coming to Light, An Advent Progress premiered at the Northampton Center for the Arts in Northampton, Massachusetts on December 14, 2019.

Contents

Green

Blue

Pace, Pacem

This is my chance to talk to you directly, in a way different from the poems that follow, and by way of introduction to them. I've been waiting for this chance for quite a while, waiting for you, somewhat like Walt Whitman in the last line of "Song of Myself"— indeed, "I stop some where waiting for you." When students and I used to read and discuss what Whitman was offering at the end of his poem, we often came around to the idea, or feeling, of how good it was for someone to "wait for us." Or, even better, to "be there for us."

Whitman, more fully, was imagining a time when he would no longer be living:

> I bequeath myself to the dirt to grow from the grass I love,
> If you want me again look for me under your bootsoles.
>
> You will hardly know who I am or what I mean,
> But I shall be good health to you nevertheless,
> And filter and fibre your blood.
>
> Failing to fetch me at first keep encouraged,
> Missing me one place search another,
> I stop some where waiting for you

How wonderful it would be to be "some where" together; then the talking would be truly direct, and it would be a matter of "with" not "to." That's not possible, of course, in the great majority of cases for poets and their *aud*ience, those who would *hear* them. But talking and hearing, or speaking and listening, were the only way of sharing for tens or hundreds of thousands of years before humankind's arguably greatest invention—not the wheel or any other technology—but the invention of *written language.* So "oral literature" expanded to written literature, that which could be shared beyond a common space. How truly wonderful to recreate life in that new way. The *re-creation* is completed when the reader imagines with the poet in the sharing about life, and in the sharing *of* life.

I think people, writers as well as readers, can often forget, overlook, or even never give any thought at all to this element of shared experience, of imagining, of recreating, *together.* And there can be a great deal to imagine; from the reader's perspective, not just the work of literature, but also the person who is providing it, who is speaking. There's a *voice* there, a voice to be *heard*, keeping in mind the essential nature of language and the far longer oral tradition of literature. And it's no disembodied voice. It is or should be full-bodied, however absent or distant it may be.

From a writer's perspective, this particular writer has spent and continues to spend a great deal of time imagining *you*, the reader. *Sharing* requires that. On one extreme hand, I wouldn't want to frustrate you or anybody beyond all reason. And, on the other, I wouldn't want to tell you in a familiar way what you already know and feel so well. What would be the point in either case?

Since there are obviously all kinds of readers (also known as "people"), how widely can I or should I try to imagine? That's the challenge. For me, like Whitman, it's important to strive to be inclusive, to leave no one out, to be democratic.

To be specific with respect to the poems in this collection, I knew that the first readers with whom I circulated the poems would be family members, friends, associates, and pretty good acquaintances—most of whom rarely, if ever, read any poetry, and many of whom did not care for poetry, or even had an aversion to it for different reasons. But I imagined as well a wider audience, strangers, both a "general reading public" and also sophisticated readers and writers of poetry, including professional poets—a good number of whom would likely have different or even opposing ideas about the nature of poetry with respect to the relative position of the poet, the poetic work, and the audience. Receptivity, acceptance, or "success" with the first broad group, more or less intimates, has gone beyond any obligatory politeness, has in fact proven encouraging. With respect to strangers, at least the sophisticated branch, a number of these poems have been submitted to magazines, published, and received a favorable response. So, the next step was to collect the separate poems for the larger sharing endeavor of a collection, an advent, if you will. Just how much of an advent would there be? How new, how old, and how much acceptance to be gained? That involves your part in the sharing, in the imagining.

The poems contain my voice, in different forms (my overall *presence*), but they must now, to use an old expression, "speak for themselves." So be it, naturally. But from this point, if you care to follow me, I think it is important to examine further the whole matter of *sharing* with poetry.

Three recent sharing experiences, of a sort, coming hard upon one another, spring to mind. First, a public poetry reading, for which there were twenty sign-up slots of five minutes each to fall within two hours. It began with the organizer's setting the scene with his own very recent composition featuring a series of "You've come to this poetry reading because . . ." followed by the proffering of images from the mundane to the intended transcendent. I lost count of the "becauses"; they were many.

The great majority of the readers who followed expressed themselves in similar open form. There were fine moments, marked by fine images. Most of the poems were narrative, seemingly the sharing of personal experience, highly earnest, quite serious and sincere, looking to lead to a profound point or effect. Several readers, either because they were nervous, or because their focus was on their personal world, or both, were turned inward, reading fast and low, making it hard for the audience to hear and connect.

One woman topped the organizer's *one* very recent composition by offering *three* that she had written that conference week. Most memorable, though, was the fellow who offered six or more poems (going well beyond the five-minute limit) and who gave after each work such an intense, beaming, expectant, even demanding look at his listeners—at once bending towards us from the waist, spreading his arms wide to engulf us, and, in fact or feeling, stomping a foot to punctuate his performance, like a plate spinner or juggler after each especially marvelous feat on the old Ed Sullivan show, all to the effect of "How about THAT!?"—or, even more to the point, "How about ME!?" He was most emphatic at the conclusion of his poem about his ex-wife's divorcing him. How could she? Poor fellow. One could only wonder.

(By way of passing comparison, at another, more formal reading held at the Academy of Music in Northampton, MA some years ago, Richard Wilbur, 90 or so at the time and still going strong, unsuspectingly got caught in an even greater "performance artist" scene, a veritable "poetry slam." He later shared with me, in great humor, his surprise over what had unfolded. He himself was slotted for a time just before intermission, and he read five poems, including "The Writer," "The Barred Owl," and "A Late Aubade," all of which stood forth as a still point in the churning world of that slam. At the end of the whole shebang, the planned headliner certainly made quite a show of himself.)

The second sharing of a sort was a poetry festival at the Emily Dickinson Museum, in particular a panel discussion by three published poets entitled "The Place You'd Like to Go: Demystifying Submissions and the Publication Process." All three hailed the advantages of nearly universal online submissions to magazines (*The Paris Review* was a noted laggard in the transition from paper to cyberspace), making it possible to whip out submissions at a far greater rate than by standard mail (which one of the poets unoriginally pooh-poohed as "snail mail"). One extoller topped the others in submission rate: over a thousand in the past five years. Her acceptance rate at the start was about five percent, but now it was up to twenty. She also shared about her participation in a writing-a-poem-a-day-for-thirty-days activity.

But that was further topped by another's being able to write, and subsequently publish, a poem in twenty minutes. The third poet, the anti-snail mailer, was also a small, very small, college magazine editor who looked for poems that were "more optimistic, grounded with concrete images, and narrative" in type—and that eschewed rhyming because of the way such sounding got in the way of meaning, according to her. She was, as were the other two, oblivious to the moldering host poet's (old Emily's) own formalist bent—and achievement.

And the third sharing experience of a sort, learned about by picking up a copy of *Poets & Writers* magazine, involved the offering of thousands and thousands of dollars in prize money (drawn from thousands more collected in submission "fees") in an astounding proliferation of contests run by magazines across the country, the great majority of which share a bias against any smack of traditional form. A reported typical rejection piece: "One note, which might go without saying, but just in case: The fact that we didn't choose to publish [the various submitters' efforts] should not be considered a ruling on their . . . merit. Poetry is always subjective, and our decision reflects nothing more than our honest fair opinion of which poems we liked most." Such reassuring critical judgment. David Hume, exhumed, might suggest another way to weigh efforts. Then, too, a lottery might also be more "objective," or just. That last possibility could be the default for poetry "judges" like the ones quoted, considering what commentator par excellence Helen Vendler has observed: "Those who suppose there are no criteria for such judgments merely expose their own incapacity."

I have called these cases "sharing experiences of a sort" because they are a sort that are lacking in important ways, as should be evident. I would not be so foolish as to hold these experiences up as a generalized reflection of the "state of poetry" or the "nature of poetry" in the United States in the early twenty-first century, although they do contain some common, easily recognizable elements. Actually, a fourth sharing experience of a sort—*and* a holding forth on the state of poetry at the same time—unfolded (also hard upon these first three cases) with the appearance of Ben Lerner's *The Hatred of Poetry* and the responses it calculatingly, commercially, provoked. Essentially, Lerner's view of poetry, at least for our time, is that it promises transcendence, but can't escape our mundane, even tragic world, or so Ken Chen, the reviewer in *The New Republic*, represented Lerner's view. The arguments of both Lerner and Chen are riddled with assumptions and reductions, with begging the question and either/or fallacies. Chen, in addition, reveals his ideological bent, that of cultural studies literary theory, with a measure of identity politics of the dividing rather than bridging sort thrown in, labeling Lerner a "conservative" on four occasions and discussing him as such throughout. Hume, again, might help here with critical judgment, especially with respect to confusions over the meanings of terms. Then, too, Gulley Jimson/Joyce Cary might be of even greater help. To "crickets" and "biogrubbers," he might have added, if living past the 1950s, "tearists." That is, those theorists who would *tear* literature apart, *scientize* it, *determinize* it, remove it from authorial will or unwilled imagination, the ultimate dark energy. If only they could.

Charles Simic, poet first, critic on occasion second, and thankfully no theorist whatsoever, gave a much more reasonable consideration of Lerner's book in *The New York Review of Books*. In response to Lerner's "theory of the impossibility of poetry," Simic offers, "While a feeling of impotence paralyzes anyone who becomes fixated on language and starts thinking about finding the right word not as an aesthetic problem, but as a theological one, it's a false quandary. Lerner fails to mention the part that poetic images, metaphors, and symbols play in circumventing the limitations of language." Or, at once more broadly and more specifically: "American poetry is a kind of do-it-yourself metaphysics. If we have a tradition in poetry—and we do—it goes back to the Transcendentalists and their empirical approach to experience, the idea that you eschew abstractions and begin with something concrete, what William Carlos Williams called 'no ideas but in things.' After that, you are on your own."

Simic and Chen both recognized Lerner's referencing or building upon Mark Edmundson's view of a decline in American poetry, due in large part to an absence of a grand vision, in his essay "Poetry Slam" in *Harper's* a few years before, an argument that, starting with its title, was guaranteed to create its own stir. One particularly unfortunate piece of "evidence" for Edmundson's own assumption-based position about what poetry should do or be was Shelley's "Ode to the West Wind," where Shelley offered, "Oh, lift me as a wave, a leaf, a cloud! / I fall upon the thorns of life! I bleed!"—and then ended by appointing, or anointing, himself messiah.

Of course, grand or special visions do not require grand scale, witness Wordsworth's "Though nothing can bring back the hour / Of splendor in the grass, of glory in the flower," Blake's "To see a World in a Grain of Sand / And a Heaven in a Wild Flower," or, perhaps better yet, Simic's point, in a previous review of books by Billy Collins and James Tate, that dealing with "a hot dog on a bun" can do quite nicely, thank you. Best of all, there is and always will be the extraordinary "ordinariness" of Shakespeare—"a willed ordinariness, a determination . . . to see the world as it is," possessing "a matchless all-sidedness and negative capability," as Adam Gopnik so trenchantly recognized in his review of Stephen Greenblatt's *Will in the World* in *The New Yorker*, concluding, "As readers and writers, we remain blessed that the reigning poet of the language is so vocationally, so happily, the ordinary poet of our company."

At the same time, what Edmundson (and Lerner also) got right beyond any grandly scaled vision was *the need for poetry to do something for readers*, to be "of our company," and that is about true sharing. My own offering here will not be *Edmundson Part Deux*, although I will make use of him. He identifies three "qualities" that would make for "superb lyric poetry," first, essentially, the gift of poetic expression (*how* or strategies), "something to say" (*what* or idea), and writing for readers (*to whom* or audience)— as opposed to writing for oneself. This is <u>not</u> about rhetoric; it's about the essential nature of language or communication, albeit on a higher plane or deeper level. If one major trend in poetry writing is to deal narratively with a string of images in free verse leading to some seemingly profound point or pearl of wisdom (an apt cliché, but it's a simulated pearl, not even a cultured one), a type written very commonly and appearing frequently in many minor publications—then a would-be higher trend is to write in highly hard-to-follow, loosely-associative (or completely-unloosed), and often fragmented or fractured ways to reach some elusive-to-the-point-of-fully-escaped private sense of some sort. Phew! Edmundson himself makes recourse to descriptors like "oblique, equivocal, painfully self-questioning," "ever more private, idiosyncratic, and withdrawn," "the obscure, the recondite, the precious," and even "programmatically obscure" with "The obvious result . . . that they shut out the common reader."

This is not news, of course, although rebroadcast here in obviously critical terms. We may be past the "confessional" categorizing of the 1950s-1970s, but it's commonly understood that most of our major and would-be major poets are on private paths, so much so that Dan Chiasson can write in a review of Robert Pinsky's *Selected*

Poems, "Pinsky is a 'public poet,' as everyone always says." Aren't poets by definition, by origin and continuation, by sheer existence, public? Of course, Chiasson goes on to focus on subject matter, on Pinsky's "meeting American mass culture halfway," neglecting the public *as in audience*—that is, the idea of speaking to the public.

And this private way can shut out as uncommon a reader as the highly insightful Vendler, for example in her holding "that [John] Ashbery does make sense if we can tune our mind to his wavelength—something I am not always able to do." But she does find it "exhilarating when that precarious harmony of minds is reached." She argues for patience with such private and occasionally impossible difficulty, rejects out-of-hand any consideration of "accessibility" in critical judgment, and claims that "Whenever an undeniably original poet appears—Mallarmé, Eliot, Moore, Milosz, Ashbery—no matter how alien the content, or how allusive the lines, readers flock to the poems." Flock as in sheep? This group of poets surely represents good company, but different sizes of flocks seem to be involved, the last-listed's being limited, again, by that particularly "precarious" quality. Maybe, then, mountain sheep? Or goats?

Then there is a reviewer like Charlotte Shane, who begins her piece "Anne Carson's Splintered Brilliance: On the Pleasures of Poetry That Deliberately Defies Our Comprehension" in *The New Republic* in this way: "I love Anne Carson's work dearly though I suspect I am too stupid for it." And ends this way: "an experience of our own stupidity, then, is a privilege afforded to us by the best art and maybe especially by the best poetry. We are granted the opportunity to swim a lap in the pool of someone else's brain, if we can." Private poet, indeed. Perhaps we wake to drowning, or get dragged up like a youthful Billy Pilgrim and emit an "um," if not "glug." Or "And so on"? But, in between, Shane offers these comforts: "Carson herself has said of her writing, 'i feel i am blundering in concepts too fine for me [sic].'" And: "Caron's [sic] admitted to using a random integer generator in her work and embracing accidental formatting changes, explaining 'it saves you a lot of worry.' She practices intentional unintentionality [sic]." And: "The unordered booklets . . . [of *Float*] evince internal derangement, too." And: "She's trafficked in fragmentation for a long time . . . Carson dwells in a space of disintegration because she doubts the existence of a cohesive whole." And so on.

It's actually a broader "and so on" that's been going on for a long, long time. Pick a starting date or historical-cultural time. WWI and the resulting fragmentation, the sense of betrayal by false institutions and false words/ideas/ideals, the "alienation of the individual," as textbooks would have it? The subsequent full emergence of existentialism and "we all die alone" (although weapons of mass destruction and some inclusion of moral concerns have tempered that view)?

But both before and after all that, haven't we also had focusing on the inner vs. the outer, the Freudian id and ego, the authentic self and the social self, the true you and the assumed you? Personally, I'm at a point where I could do with a little less of private worlds and more with the public one involving sensitivity to and caring for others. Otherwise, we make a complete shift from "and so on" to the (ever increasing) death march of "So it goes." Nota bene: the Science and Security Board of the *Bulletin of the Atomic Scientists* decided in January 2017 "to move the minute hand of the Doomsday Clock 30 seconds closer to catastrophe. It is now two minutes and 30 seconds to midnight. The board's decision . . . reflects a simple reality: As this statement is issued, Donald Trump has been the US president only a matter of days." The implication with respect to subsequent developments is obvious.

We could skip back hundreds of years to the early Renaissance and the Reformation in the West, to the beginning of modern valuing of the individual. So much of modern history, in fact, can be seen as being about the rise of the individual (none of that ultra-communitarian "The nail that sticks up must be hammered down"). Nowhere is this more true than in the US with our focus on individual freedom. We all are born wanting to be free, to do what we want to do and be who or what we want to be, "conceived in liberty," as Lincoln would have it, both as a nation and as individuals.

But we've always struggled with equality, with others being as valued or important as ourselves. Emerson, Thoreau, and Whitman understood that our individualism <u>was not</u>, and <u>must not be</u>, narcissism—that our individualism transcendentally, democratically, and poetically connected us all as essentially equal: "I celebrate myself, / And what I assume you shall assume, / For every atom belonging to me as good belongs to you." Lincoln wisely recognized that equality was a proposition (a nation "dedicated to the proposition that all men are created equal"), an idea, an argument, that all people are or should be equally free, equally important, equally treated. He called for a "new birth of freedom" for *all*. The nation was being supremely tested. Democracy—the idea that a society could organize itself so that everyone was free <u>and</u> equal—was at stake. It's still at stake. The test isn't over yet. Even the war isn't over yet. More than ever, the question is whether such a nation will "perish." The state of democracy and the state of life itself are in a far more precarious position than that of being in harmony with some private poet.

Many otherwise-wise people have looked down upon all those

who voted for Trump for president—those "Trumpists," that largely "forgotten white working class," or the millions of "deplorables" involved therein. George Packer traced this distancing problem from 1968 to the threshold of the election in "The Unconnected: The Democrats Lost the White Working Class. The Republicans Exploited Them. Can Hillary Clinton Win Them Back?" in the October 31, 2016 *The New Yorker*. No, she couldn't. Packer wrote the best "post-election analysis" before the election had even occurred. A failure to connect, a failure to empathize, a tendency to elitism had grown over time and even now continues to be wrestled with. But what does that state of the country have to do with the state of poetry? It's the same distancing problem, the same disconnect, and the wrestling has yet to truly begin. We're more or less poetically stuck in post-WWI alienation. As Glyn Maxwell writes in *On Poetry*,

> Is the young poet *still* to feel hurtled into a jagged new zone of speed and fuel and skyscrapers and faceless strangers? Is it still the future? Are we still so alienated? . . . my strong suspicion remains that many young writers of the late 20th century, particularly in the West, developed styles and strategies of verse that were not an effect of social or political reality . . . so much as of literary history, or, to be less charitable, aesthetic inclination, that the once-vital, visceral responses of early Modernism have dwindled over a hundred years into thoroughly private habits.

It's time to become "unstuck in time." In simplest terms, courtesy of E. M. Forster, "Only connect."

So much of the cultural-literary mindset of the past 100+ years, at least in the US, has been about connecting with oneself, not with others. With all of the alienation and social meaning-lessness, it was incumbent upon the individual to rid himself/her-self of romantic illusions and create his/her own meaning in life. So it came about that the "lost generation" and succeeding generations fell prey to their own, individual romanticism, what E. L. Doctorow has called being "in thrall to the romance of the self." Or as Wilbur has commented, at least about the confessional mode of this excessive inwardness,

> I do feel that the truth, especially the truth about oneself, is hard to report, and that if you set out to confess, what you are likely to do is tell lies in addition to reporting some of the truth. And the fact that you are consciously part of the material of the poem may lead you to falsify in ways that are not good. There are good fictions and bad fictions. The kind of fiction that glamorizes you is not good either for your sake or for the reader's, and I think that very often the confessional poet is drawn to glamorize himself, whether he is aware of it or not.

Years before Packer's "The Unconnected" dealing with our sociopolitical scene, he blogged about trying to convince then president-elect Obama not to have a poem read at his inauguration: "For many decades American poetry has been a private activity, written by few people and read by few people, lacking the language, rhythm, emotion, and thought that could move large numbers of people in large public settings." Simic, referring to Lerner's quoting of this blog, aims for a strong rebuttal:

> Packer seems to be as uninformed about the United States as he can be about the Middle East and the rest of the world. Poetry readings,

with crowds sometimes numbering into hundreds, have been a staple of colleges and universities for the last fifty years, with those taking place in New York City listed in the magazine he works for. Those who attend them do so eagerly and clearly enjoy themselves, because they keep coming back. They hear a great variety of poets and even purchase their books afterward. To be acquainted with something so common-place and still pontificate on a subject one knows nothing about is what all those who disparage poetry sound like.

This response is both unmeasured and self-defeating. And it's partly sidetracked by "public settings," not to mention the light-weight of "hundreds." The real issue is about "private activity." Simic immediately follows with a "more substantial objection" raised by Edmundson, as cited by Lerner. Simic quotes Edmundson, "They ["contemporary poets"] don't slake a reader's thirst for meanings that pass beyond the experience of the individual poet and light up the world we hold in common," and Simic comments, "In other words, they have become too self-absorbed to notice other people. Edmundson has a point, of course." And it's very much in the vein of Packer.

Simic's own poetry is not of the highly private and fragmented sort. The poetics he expresses in his Billy Collins and James Tate review in the *NYRB* is that ". . . there has to be a countercurrent; a touch of ambiguity and uncertainty as it were. Not the kind that leads nowhere and makes the reader give up on the poem in no time, but the kind that draws us back into it. What one needs is some unexpected image or twist in the point of view that makes us realize that there's more here than meets the eye."

Beyond contending views about the relative privacy of poetry, there certainly is considerable data, both statistical through extensive research and anecdotal through compelling testimony, that the general reading of poetry continues in sharp decline (second only to reading plays in the overall decline in literary reading, within the greater context of the fall-off in arts participation overall).[1] And that comes, not coincidentally, amid similar research and testimony about the falling away of empathy. Writer Caryl Phillips made a strong connection between the two areas in a 2010 radio interview that marked the end of his year in residence at the University of Massachusetts in Amherst:

> The biggest change is that students don't read as much. Which is kind of worrying. They don't read. . . . We live in an age where they're not supposed to *sympathize* with people. You vote them off the island, you vote them out of the house, you laugh at them on *The American Idol*, you know. The empathy with other people, the very bedrock, if you like, of the imagination, literature, understanding people who are not you, including immigrants, people who are in exile, people who are suffering—the culture seems to have moved away from that . . .

With respect to the poetry part of literature, before we can expect readers to connect with others, to have empathy for others,

---

1 The National Endowment for the Arts did offer some qualified excitement in June 2018 about its 2017 survey results showing a rise in poetry reading, approaching what it had been in 2002. There had been a steady decline since 1992. Initial analysis about possible causes for the rise centered on the emergence of "social media . . . as well as other robust outreach activities and efforts," including the NEA's Poetry Out Loud program among students in all 50 states and its Big Read program in 75 communities across the country. One may naturally wonder about the depth of this participation. And about its self-sustainability.

to try to do more than gain some access to the hermetic world of a private poet, it would make sense for the writer of poetry to do more to connect with readers—and to connect with *more* readers in and of themselves. That is, to go well beyond critics (a target audience for private poets, Edmundson suspects) or beyond an exclusive club of likeminded poets and partakers. In other words, the idea is for a poet to have empathy, or greater empathy, for readers, for so-called common readers. A natural reaction might be, "Why should I do that? Why should I pander or compromise myself? Or how can I do that when I'm pursuing matter that is elusive enough for me as a writer? How can I make it 'accessible' [that word again] for readers? And how large a set of readers are we talking about, how *public* the public, how general, how inclusive—inclusive even of the disaffected, the antagonistic, the 'deplorables'?"

But before trying to answer questions like these, perhaps the poet needs to ask himself/herself some questions, like "For whom am I writing this poem in particular or my poems in general—*really*? Primarily for myself? Partly for myself? For an elite group? For posterity? For those who will, if not now then sometime in the future, realize that I have reached heights, or depths, not previously reached in the past 2500 years or so? As we are now crossing into *purpose* (another essential element of language/communication), what is my purpose for a particular poem or my poetry? To satisfy the tastes (biases?) of a particular audience, or a particular magazine or set of magazines? Am I trying to achieve some greater purpose with respect to an audience—what do I hope to do *for them*, if anything at all? Am I ultimately, by necessity, faced with an either/or proposition (fallacy?)—them or me? Or my art vs. the public, or a larger public? Some degree of exclusion at least vs. an all-inclusiveness?

It always does come down to self and (vs.?) others, doesn't it? Consider this passage from Forster's *A Passage to India* about inviting natives to a 1920s British Raj tea party with a "bridge" purpose:

And there were circles even beyond these—people who wore nothing but a loin-cloth, people who wore not even that, and spent their lives in knocking two sticks together before a scarlet doll—humanity grading and drifting beyond the educated vision, until no earthly invitation can embrace it.

All invitations must proceed from heaven perhaps; perhaps it is futile for men to initiate their own unity, they do but widen the gulfs between them by the attempt. So at all events thought old Mr. Graysford and young Mr. Sorley, the devoted missionaries who lived out beyond the slaughterhouses, always traveled third on the railways, and never came to the club. In our Father's house are many mansions, they taught, and there alone will the incompatible multitudes of mankind be welcomed and soothed. Not one shall be turned away by the servants on that verandah, be he black or white, not one shall be kept standing who approaches with a loving heart. And why should the divine hospitality cease here? Consider, with all reverence, the monkeys. May there not be a mansion for the monkeys also? Old Mr. Graysford said No, but young Mr. Sorley, who was advanced, said Yes; he saw no reason why monkeys should not have their collateral share of bliss, and he had sympathetic discussions about them with his Hindu friends. And the jackals? Jackals were indeed less to Mr. Sorley's mind but he admitted that the mercy of God, being infinite, may well embrace all mammals. And the wasps? He became uneasy during the descent to wasps, and was apt to change the conversation. And oranges, cactuses, crystals and mud? and the bacteria inside Mr. Sorley? No, no, this is going too far. We must exclude someone from our gathering, or we shall be left with nothing.

So, there must be exclusion in the far narrower celestial realm of poetry? But *must* there be, really? Is it really an either/or proposition, or might it be possible to strike a balance among poet, audience, and some purpose/meaning? But how encompass the ignorant, the disaffected, the antagonistic, those without "a loving heart"? How pull them in? Is failure certain or almost certain? Are we back to a Lerner view of poetry as failure, in particular in the person of Whitman, "the paradigmatic, but unsuccessful, poet of American radical inclusivity," to use Chen's capsulizing?

But how do you measure success? Could there ever be a perfect inclusiveness, a perfect equality, a perfect democracy, a perfect union, on earth? Are ideals ever made real? No, of course not. So is the "real" alternative to give up? Surrender? Be hopeless? But remember what really is at stake at this time with respect to democracy and to survival itself. Consider what Arthur Miller came to in the struggle over self vs. others in *The Crucible*, particularly in Proctor's confronting Judge Danforth: "A fire, a fire is burning! I hear the boot of Lucifer, I see his filthy face! And it is my face, and yours, Danforth! For them that quail to bring men out of ignorance, as I have quailed, and as you quail now when you know in all your black hearts that this be fraud—God damns our kind especially, and we will burn, we will burn together!" Proctor ends up making an *individual, free choice for the sake of the lives and souls of others—and, at the same time, for the sake of his own soul.* Yes, he is hung for it. But the fear-mongering and hysteria and hatred are beaten back, in 1692 and in 1954. And now?

And was Whitman "unsuccessful"? Isn't he still out there, "waiting"? And didn't he achieve a great deal? Don't we return to him again and again? And wasn't Thoreau right, "For it matters not how small the beginning may seem to be: what is once well done is done forever"? Were Douglass, Lincoln, King, and Gandhi without success?

Clearly, poets historically come to grief with audiences, the greater the grief met as a result of the greater the audience aimed for. Witness the experiences of poets as diverse as William Blake ("What is Grand is necessarily obscure to Weak men. That which can be made Explicit to the Idiot is not worthy my care," writing to Dr. Truster), W. B. Yeats (e.g., "Adam's Curse"), Dylan Thomas (e.g., "In My Craft or Sullen Art"), and William Carlos Williams (e.g., "Tract"). Then, too, our "reigning poet," the "ordinary poet of our company," continuously wrestled with this audience matter, yet managed to make his way quite well in "writing for the masses" and being "the most popular entertainer of his day," as is commonly recognized. In all of the instances in which he addressed the lowbrow as well as the middle and the high, perhaps the most direct with respect to the low occurs in *Julius Caesar*: "You blocks, you stones, you worse than senseless things." Of course, the cobbler and his fellow "knaves" or working class "mechanicals" get the better of their seeming betters, two tribunes, at the very outset of the play, that is, at least until Flavius and Marullus authoritatively disperse them. But those two foreshadow the out-of-touch, proud high-mindedness of Brutus that brings him down. They themselves "are put to silence," Casca reports, "for pulling scarfs off Caesar's images" long before Brutus conspires and subsequently falls. Also, we shouldn't overlook the fate of the uninvolved, distant, removed Cinna the Poet when he encounters by chance the masses once they have been enflamed by a demagogue's (Antony's) rhetoric:

> *Third Plebeian.* Your name, sir, truly.
> *Cinna.* Truly, my name is Cinna.
> *First Plebeian.* Tear him to pieces! He's a conspirator.
> *Cinna.* I am Cinna the poet! I am Cinna the poet!
> *Fourth Plebeian.* Tear him for his bad verses! Tear him for his bad verses!
> *Cinna.* I am not Cinna the conspirator.
> *Fourth Plebeian.* It is no matter, his name's Cinna; pluck but his name out of his heart, and turn him going.
> *Third Plebeian.* Tear him, tear him! [*They attack him.*]

Such is the "removal" of Cinna the Poet. But there is still another poet, one who oddly appears at the armed camp of Brutus and Cassius and tries to get "involved" too late, during the big kerfuffle between the two major conspirators:

> *Poet.* Let me go to see the generals;
> There is some grudge between 'em; 'tis not meet
> They be alone.
> *Lucilius.* You shall not come to them.
> *Poet.* Nothing but death shall stay me.
> *Cassius.* How now. What's the matter?
> *Poet.* For shame, you generals! What do you mean?
> Love, and be friends, as two such men should be;
> For I have seen more years, I'm sure, than ye.

Cassius. Ha, ha! How vilely doth the cynic [boor] rhyme!

Brutus. Get you home, sirrah! Saucy fellow, hence!

Cassius. Bear with him, Brutus, 'tis his fashion.

Brutus. I'll know his humor when he knows his time.
  What should the wars do with these jigging fools?
  Companion, hence!

Cassius.   Away, away, be gone.

Another removal, this time with a dismissal of the poet's art if not his life. It certainly is tough for a poet to make his/her way with both the high and mighty and the low and mighty—or with a general audience—but Shakespeare showed that it could be done. "Time," or timing, is crucial, as we shall see more of.

Perhaps the earliest significant addressing of the difficulties with audience occurred with Plato in *The Republic*. Plato did <u>not</u> hate poetry, a common reductive view (cf. Lerner, Chen, Simic, many more). Plato and those like him "admire," "love," and "respect" Homer, Aeschylus, and other such poets, and he writes, "We must ask Homer and the other poets to excuse us if we delete . . . passages [that do not serve the educational purpose of the *ideal*, "Platonic," republic envisioned] . . . not that they are bad poetry or are not popular; indeed the better they are as poetry the more unsuitable they are for the ears of children or men who are to be free and fear slavery more than death." Children or the future militaristic guardians of the "ideal state" are not the only audience of concern—so, too, as indicated, are men who are "foolish" or "impressionable." Consider:

So if we are visited in our state by someone who has the skill to transform himself into all sorts of characters and represent all sorts of things, and he wants to show off himself and his poems to us, we shall treat him with all the reverence due to a priest and giver of rare pleasure, but shall tell him that he and his kind have no place in our city, their presence being forbidden by our code, and send him elsewhere, after anointing him with myrrh and crowning him with fillets of wool. For ourselves, we shall for our own good employ storytellers and poets who are severe rather than amusing, who portray the style of the good man and in their works abide by the principles we laid down for them when we started out on this attempt to educate our military class.

Plato certainly knew firsthand the turbulence, the whipping up of common people, the wars, all the deaths, including that of his beloved mentor, friend, and subsequent stand-in, Socrates, in the shifting democracy of fifth-century BCE Greece. The general public, the general "audience," "others"—that is, just plain people—are the ultimate concern, then as well as now. They can't be ignored—and they can't be left to would-be autocrats. But we today seek not an "ideal state" but as viable and as just a republic as possible.

Ironically, on one level, poets of today who tend to the private, the highly individual pursuit of some elusive truths or senses or profundities bordering on the tendentious, seem closer to Plato's idea of "direct speech of poets themselves" and the limited representation or mimesis that he preferred for his ideal state. But then, too, Plato could hardly have looked favorably upon some of the personal or direct speech phenomena of our day, that is, the oxymoronic proliferation of prefabricated memoirs, "creative nonfiction," and reality TV. Hardly ideal.

As for style with respect to the poets to be excluded by Plato from his ideal state—that is, those who would be inclusive of the world as it is at large—he expects that from them "We shall have the noises of thunder and wind and hail, and of axles and wheels, the notes of trumpets, pipes, flutes, and every possible instrument, the barking of dogs, the baaing of sheep, and twittering of birds."

As for the preferred poets speaking directly for themselves, the style would be "pretty uniform, given music of appropriate mode and rhythm to accompany it ["severe rather than amusing" or pleasurable]. In fact if one handles it rightly one and the same mode and harmony can be employed throughout, because of the uniformity of the style . . ." Plato's preferred uniform style bears something in common to the supposedly individual yet commonly followed style or "voice" frequently raised up as a praiseworthy achievement in our time.

Plato rounds off with the other, the style to be rejected: "The other style, on the other hand, will have the opposite requirements. It will need every kind of mode, and every kind of rhythm, if it is to find suitable expression, as its variety of change is unlimited." But since "all poets and speakers [must] go in for one or other of these two styles or some combination of them," there is a choice to be made. Plato in the character of Socrates recognizes that "the combination of the two styles is very pleasant, and the opposite style [to the severe one advocated] . . . gives most pleasure to . . . the general public." But since a safe, protected, ideal state is the goal, the limited style is chosen.

Shakespeare, the great comprehensive "ordinary poet of our company," chose in favor of our *ordinary* state, our *ordinary* world, "transform[ing] himself into all sorts of characters and represent[ing] all sorts of things," dealing in "every kind of mode, and every kind of rhythm," ranging over a poetry-prose continuum, but always essentially rhythmic. He does favor iambic rhythm, particularly in pentameter length, because he recognizes the essentially binary tonal nature of the English language (all of the ups and downs, a natural cadence in itself), the roots of poetry in song, and the strength of a more focused, song-like rhythm for conveying sense strongly.

What, then, is Shakespeare's "voice"? He has no one voice. That's the point. That's his achievement. He's all voices and all things. He doesn't have one authorial or poet's "voice" in the increasingly self-focused or self-absorbed view of the past 100+ years. What he does have is a great *presence*, an *authorial presence*, an abiding presence that we get strong senses of but can't figure out or nail down in terms of a specific, individual person. Many people for the longest time have been desperate to do just that with him, as if that is what really mattered. It's as if many had a need for a personality cult or hero worship or groupie following. But Shakespeare's achievement is not about *who* he was but about *what* he did, *how* he did it, and about *for whom* he did it. It's about art, about poetry specifically.

We can't figure out Shakespeare individually because his presence is universal, eternal. Keats understood that about Shakespeare and about poetry. We would all benefit from looking to Keats's understanding. In one of his many insightful comments about poetry in his letters, this one addressed to his friend John Hamilton Reynolds, he moves from personal affairs to the approach of Shakespeare's birthday:

> Tell George and Tom [Keats's brothers] to write.—I'll tell what—On the 23rd was Shakespeare born—now If I should receive

a Letter from you and another from my Brothers on that day 'twould be a parlous good thing—Whenever you write say a Word or two on some Passage in Shakespeare that may have come rather new to you; which must be continually happening, notwithstand that we read the same Play forty times . . . [quoting from *The Tempest*] I find that I cannot exist without poetry—without eternal poetry . . .

That's Simic's idea of "draws us back," but in a multifold, continuing way. That's not *the facile* or *the obscure*, the two great trends in modern poetry referred to earlier. No, it's the endlessly rich, a sharing that we then share among ourselves, as Keats vibrantly demonstrates.

The contemporary view of voice is another matter entirely from what this preface began with. That contemporary view is focused on the poet, on him or her in what's written. Louise Gluck, in her regularly recalled introduction to *The Best American Poetry 1993*, offers,

> The world is complete without us. Intolerable fact. To which the poet responds by rebelling, writing to prove otherwise. Out of wounded vanity or stubborn pride or desolate need, the poet lives in chronic dispute with fact . . . The poem, no matter how charged its content, survives not through content but through voice. By voice I mean style of thought . . . it [voice] suggests, at least, the sound of an authentic being . . . unlike speech, it bears no immediate social pressure, since the other to whom it strives to make itself clear may not yet exist. The poem means to create that person, first in the poet, then in the reader. Meanwhile, its fidelity is not to external reality: it need not provide a replica of the outward, or of social relations. . . . Poems *are* autobiography . . .

Vendler, in a related way, states that "individual human uniqueness [is] the quality most prized in artists, and most salient, and most valued, in the arts." There is no art without the artist, surely, at least not yet in our increasingly electronic world, but for an artist, a poet, to be elevated to this extent? "Vanity"? "Pride"? Or at least a balance lost or tipped? We may well weigh Yeats's "How can we know the dancer from the dance?" But a loss or lack of balance will make us know readily and detract from the dance. And it is the dance itself that brings us audience members in. And we must be brought in. There is no dance without us. And a dancer who does not exist yet, or one who wishes to be glamorized or idolized apart from the dance? That just will not do.

One of the truly great books about poetry—I would say not just intellectually wholesome, but spiritually as well (far outdistancing the Gideon and perhaps rivaling the KJB)—is Jay Parini's *Why Poetry Matters*, but he, too, gets caught up, or catches himself up, in individual voice as the ultimate matter for poets:

> The complex issue of voice . . . obsesses poets. Young poets try to cultivate their own voice. But what exactly is this magical thing, its gold panned for in the stream of common language? . . . How does a poet's voice relate to the development of his or her persona or mask: the self that is created through language? I will argue in these pages that poetry matters, in part, because of voice.

At least the qualifier "in part." But once again, Shakespeare and other great poets do not "cultivate" a "voice." They do not don a mask-self. They emerge *naturally* and at the deeper level of *presence*. Parini, to his significant credit, analyzes at great length his sense of "voice" and seeks to ground his analysis by making particular use of Yeats, Frost, Stevens, and Eliot, frequently referring to their donning of "masks" on the path to arriving finally at their own "voices." But the word "masks" can be misleading, suggesting a falseness, a limitation, an apartness rather than a true inhabiting, an empathy, as understood above from Plato to Shakespeare. His final view of Frost pulls matters together, more or less:

> Frost uses masks not to deflect the personal voice but to find one, or several. He speaks truthfully when speaking as someone else, when he can assume the otherness of a mask, looking through those eyeholes at the world. . . . Paradoxically, it seems harder to speak as oneself without the sustained practice of speaking as someone else. . . .
>
> By the time Frost composed ["The Road Not Taken"], he had practiced himself in different voices for many years, and found what felt right and true. Of course, Frost was inventing himself, using a mask, even when speaking supposedly as himself. One must *never* confuse the "I" of a lyric poem with the poet; the "I" is just an eye, or two eyeholes poked through a makeshift construction. But if Frost sounds remarkably fresh, colloquial, and authentic in his lyric poems, this has as much to do with being acquainted with otherness by having tried on so many guises, by having worn the antithetical uniform of other selves self-consciously, even bravely. He learned how to speak in another's voice so that in those moments of sublime self-revelation one covets in literary texts, he could speak as himself as well. [cf. Vendler above]

This sounds very nice in a way, especially the attention to "otherness," but it contains claims without evidence and with quite a bit of muddle. The self is also a mask, but then there is self-revelation?

And how do we know that? And "one covets" that revealing of self "in literary texts"? This "one" doesn't so covet, and I don't know other "ones" who do either. We want as much of the world, of life—depth even more than breadth—as we can get. We want the life of the art, far more than the life of the artist.

The driving force for all this focus on "voice," self, or the personal, according to Parini, is that familiar period, once again, starting back in the early twentieth-century: "—a period of immense stress, when the world seemed to be coming apart, and where individuality itself seemed threatened by various mass movements and from mass culture itself, which suddenly had so many more powerful outlets for its depersonalized voice. These poets had to fight their way toward personal expression . . ." Is there not too much made of this, and for too long, especially in the 50+ years since the deaths of these four giants? Eliot, the last of "the major modern poets" Parini uses for his argument about voice, famously stated, "The progress of an artist is a continual self-sacrifice, a continual extinction of personality."

To his credit, Parini recognizes to some extent how contemporary poetry itself is largely broken, fragmented, alienated, community-lacking:

> In "A Secular Pilgrimage," [Wendell] Berry meditates on one
> of the central issues for poetry in our time. "The poetry of this cen-
> tury," he writes, "like the world in this century, has suffered from
> the schism in modern consciousness. It has been turned back upon
> itself, fragmented, obscured in its sense of its function. Like all oth-
> er human pursuits, it has had to suffer, and to some extent enact,
> the modern crisis: the failure of the past to teach us to deal with the

present or to envision and prepare for a desirable future. It has often seemed to lack wholeness and wisdom.

But Parini beats a hasty retreat (from what he has just raised) with essentially a non-response: "This is not to disparage poetry but to suggest that the field is complex, with successes and failures. Poets are human beings, and they cannot escape the problems of their time or see through all the blind spots." That's playing it safe; no offending anyone there. But the past has amply demonstrated that poets are not just "human beings" (no revelation in Parini's claim!), but ones who actually have some special gifts and who at least *try to do more for others*. However, in the past 100+ years, especially since the beginning of the nuclear age and its yawning abyss, our poets have generally turned to self-absorption. Or a self-abyss in some cases, as if that is somehow preferable.

After further calling most poets "workaday creatures who labor in the vineyards, digging their rows, planting seeds, watering the plants, harvesting what they can," Parini digs more deeply yet into the overall malaise, referring to "one of [the twentieth-century's] most vibrant philosophers," Alfred Lord Whitehead, and how he pointed to the domination of science and "a divorce of science from the affirmations of our aesthetic and ethical experiences." But Parini then falls back again: "Poetry, with its relentless concreteness and affectionate attendance on the natural world, plays a role in the restoration, giving back to readers a vision of creation in all its many dimensions." Playing a role? Not a leadership role, apparently. Restoration? Not in sight, or in the sight of many. And what about Whitehead's yoking the ethical to the aesthetic in Parini's response? Nowhere in sight.

Keats's letters are marked repeatedly by his own desire "of doing the world some good," his upholding empathy as the ultimate value, his rejecting self-absorption. From Plato to Shakespeare to Eliot and now back a step to Keats, in his letter to Richard Woodhouse:

> As to the poetical Character itself, (I mean that sort of which, if I am any thing, I am a Member; that sort distinguished from the wordsworthian or egotistical sublime; which is a thing per se and stands alone) it is not itself—it has no self—it is every thing and nothing—It has no character—it enjoys light and shade; it lives in gusto, be it foul or fair, high or low, rich or poor, mean or elevated—. . . A Poet is the most unpoetical of any thing in existence; because he has no Identity—he is continually in for—and filling some other Body—The Sun, the Moon, the Sea and Men and Women who are creatures of impulse are poetical and have about them an unchangeable attribute—the poet has none; no identity—he is certainly the most unpoetical of all God's Creatures.

Keats's letters, of course, are no formal manifesto; he explores in his thinking about poetry, but there are some constants, including more about doing good in a letter to John Taylor: "I find there is no worthy pursuit but the idea of doing some good to the world. Some do it with their society—some with their wit—some with their benevolence—some with a sort of power of conferring pleasure and good humour on all they meet—and in a thousand ways, all equally dutiful to the command of Great Nature—there is but one way for me. The road lies through application, study, and thought," and that is manifested in his poetic creation.

His exploring can take the form of wrestling over some matters, especially Wordsworth's poetry, addressed above and again in this letter to Reynolds: ". . . but for the sake of a few imaginative or domestic passages, are we to be bullied into a certain Philosophy engendered in the whims of an Egotist [?] . . ." A little later, there's some backing off: "—I don't mean to deny Wordsworth's grandeur . . . but I mean to say we need not be teazed with grandeur . . . when we can have [it] uncontaminated & unobtrusive." And in a later letter to Reynolds, he finds that Milton "did not think into the human heart, as Wordsworth has done."

Keats was right to try to view Wordsworth more justly, more broadly, not focusing alone on the older poet's ascribed "egotistical" bent. Of course, Wordsworth's aim was for connecting with larger truths or, in the words of English Romantic scholar David Perkins— for "the inner and outer . . . indissolubly blended." For quite some time now, modern inwardness alone has been commonly traced back to Wordsworth as the wellspring. Overlooked are Wordsworth's greater democratic aspirations. As he wrote in his preface to the second edition of the revolutionary *Lyrical Ballads*, "The principal object . . . proposed in these Poems was to choose incidents and situations from common life, and to relate or describe them, throughout, as far as was possible in a selection of language really used by men . . ." A further explanation from Wordsworth might well serve as a commentary on the more private practices of our time:

> . . . such a language, arising out of repeated experience and regular feelings, is a more permanent, and a far more philosophical language, than that which is frequently substituted for it by Poets, who think they are conferring honour upon themselves and their art, in proportion as they separate themselves from the sympathies

of men, and indulge in arbitrary and capricious habits of expression, in order to furnish food for fickle tastes, and fickle appetites, of their own creation.

Elsewhere in his preface, he expresses his view about language and audience in a way that would seem to fit Shane's review of Carson discussed above, allowing that a poet "might . . . use a peculiar language when expressing his feelings for his own gratification, or that of men like himself. But Poets do not write for Poets alone, but for men. Unless, therefore, we are advocates for that admiration which subsists upon ignorance, and that pleasure which arises from hearing what we do not understand, the Poet must descend from this supposed height . . ."

In his extensive discussion of language, Wordsworth firmly holds that "not only the language of a large portion of every good poem, even of the most elevated character, must necessarily, except with reference to metre, in no respect differ from that of good prose, but likewise that some of the most interesting parts of the best poems will be found to be strictly the language of prose when prose is well written." Yet, poetic expression does end up mattering more: ". . . of two expressions, either of passions, manners, or characters each of them equally well executed, the one in prose and the other in verse, the verse will be read a hundred times where the prose is read once." But stepping back a bit, how can meter be involved in "language really used by men"? A common view of free verse advocates and practitioners is that poems written in that form are closer to natural speech, actual speech; that meter or formalist practices come off as artificial, unnatural, meaning-deficient. Wordsworth seemingly anticipates this issue:

. . . as it may be proper to remind the Reader, the distinction of metre is regular and uniform, and not, like that which is produced by what is usually called POETIC DICTION, arbitrary, and subject to infinite caprices, upon which no calculation whatever can be made. In the one, the Reader is utterly at the mercy of the Poet, respecting what imagery or diction he may choose to connect with the passion; whereas, in the other, the metre obeys certain laws, to which the Poet and Reader both willingly submit because they are certain, and because no interference is made by them with the passion, but such as the concurring testimony of ages has shown to heighten and improve the pleasure which co-exists with it.

To draw upon Wordsworth in this way is not to reignite, or to continue to fan the flames of, the fiery war of "formalists" vs. "anti-formalists"—more specifically the ideologues in each camp who reject out-of-hand any verse from the other. The focus in *this* preface, again, is about poetry's being more democratic, and the fact is that sound, musical qualities, have mattered a great deal with audiences for a long, long time—Wordsworth, of course, refers to "the concurring testimony of ages."

I can readily imagine a reader squirming over or reacting against the idea that "the metre obeys certain laws, to which the Poet and Reader both willingly submit." Laws? Submit? Clearly, many want no part of any such submission. But it might be worth relating syntax at this point. Syntax, of course, deals with the laws of language dating all the way back to its origin. Syntax, the laws or rules involved in it, help define what it is to be human, distinguishing us from other species, providing an essential bond between people. Now, syntax is not always in full operation with us, especially in our minds, and writers have used broken syntax to achieve great meaning and effect, John Berryman's *Dream Songs* being a notable example. But when syntax is violently and continuously broken, when it seems utterly fractured, when all but a select few readers turn away from it—and this is a trend within the more private and wildly associative (assuming some association) vein in contemporary poetry—then one has to wonder about the lack of empathy for or connection to audience. The so-called "laws" of meter can be a further way of connecting to an audience, of bonding, especially when we consider the origins and development of poetry in shared song.

Of all of America's great poets, a strong case has repeatedly been made for Whitman as the most influential—but an equally strong case could be made for Robert Frost as the closest we have had to a national poet. And his case is not about being "accessible" since far more often than not Frost is challenging in richly ambiguous ways. No, it's more about his being welcoming with respect to language, syntax, and meter—or, if you will, his out-Wordsworthing Wordsworth. Vendler's commentary, as almost always, is astute: "Frost prided himself on having captured in poetry the 'sentence sounds' of ordinary speech." Another piece: "Frost played speech against meter, and enjoyed the way he turned the stately blank verse of Milton and Wordsworth into preposterous lines like the final sentence uttered by the aged pauper 'witch' of Grafton." Still another: "Behind all of Frost's country dialogues is the glee he felt in turning the lofty into the low, in reforming blank-verse diction far beyond what Wordsworth had done in bringing it down to the language of 'a man speaking to men.'" Finally: "And everywhere there is heard the Frostian rhythm, in which iambs interspersed with anapests and spondees manage strings of syllables mounting to barely bridled hysteria or subsiding into Yankee irony."

As for Whitman, he himself, of course, was no regularly metrical poet; instead, he became the great promoter or popularizer of free verse. But musical qualities (especially rhythm), common language, and flowing syntax were a significant part of his reaching out to readers. His repetitions—of words, especially at the beginning of lines (i.e., anaphora)—of grammatical structures (i.e., parallelism)—of sounds, or chiming (e.g., alliteration, consonance, assonance, rhyming, and half-rhyming); his building of momentum, sweep, complete musicality, or "wall-of sound" (like in "pop music," according to April Bernard); his series and sequences of phrases; and his beats, his cadence, even his occasional resorting to iambs—all of this has long been recognized and commented upon. Drawing from just two of his poems, see examples of his *sound effects*—better yet, *hear* them or *move* to them. First, "Cavalry Crossing a Ford":

> A line in long array, where they wind betwixt green islands,
> They take a serpentine course, their arms flash in the sun—hark to
> the musical clank,
> Behold the silvery river, in it the splashing horses, loitering, stop to
> drink,
> Behold the brown-faced men, each group, each person a picture,
> the negligent rest on the saddles,
> Some emerge on the opposite bank, others are just entering the
> ford—while,
> Scarlet and blue and snowy white,
> The guidon flags flutter gaily in the wind.

Then let's return to those last six lines of "Song of Myself":

> You will hardly know who I am or what I mean,
> But I shall be good health to you nevertheless,
> And filter and fibre your blood.

Failing to fetch me at first keep encouraged,

Missing me one place search another,

I stop some where waiting for you

The musical evidence is readily apparent, that is, readily audible, *heard*. I will just point to the less obvious rhythm and reversal achieved with syntax in the last three lines, the first two of which are independent clauses headed by participial phrases, the last also an independent clause but with the participial phrase coming at the end, and all of it ending at the greatest place of emphasis on "you"—with no end punctuation, no period, no end at all. How can we help being connected, poet and reader? How can we help being part of the song?

It's worth looking in brief at what Whitman had to say about more formal, regular, traditional rhyme and rhythm:

The poetic quality is not marshaled in rhyme or uniformity or abstract addresses to things nor in melancholy complaints or good precepts, but is the life of these and much else and is the soul. The profit of rhyme is that it drops seeds of a sweeter and more luxuriant rhyme, and of uniformity that it conveys itself into its own roots in the ground out of sight. The rhyme and uniformity of perfect poems show the free growth of metrical laws and bud from them as unerringly and loosely as lilacs or roses on a bush, and take shapes as compact as the shapes of chestnuts and oranges and melons and pears, and shed the perfume impalpable to form. The fluency and ornaments of the finest poems or music or orations or recitations are not independent but dependent. All beauty comes from beautiful blood and a beautiful brain. If the greatnesses are in conjunction in a man or woman it is enough . . . . the fact will prevail through the universe . . . . but the gaggery and gilt of a million years will not prevail. Who troubles himself about his ornaments or fluency is lost.

It was "the gaggery and gilt" following from making rhyme and uniformity (metrical rhythm) "independent," or of first, troubling concern—it is that which must be avoided. Whitman recognized a degeneration, or a potential for it, over a half-century before Ezra Pound did. Pound, a *Founding Father* of Modernism, held forth similarly in "Imagisme":

> Don't chop your stuff into separate *iambs*. Don't make each line stop dead at the end, and then begin every next line with a heave. Let the beginning of the next line catch the rise of the rhythm wave, unless you want a definite longish pause.
>
> In short, behave as a musician, a good musician, when dealing with that phase of your art which has exact parallels in music. The same laws govern, and you are bound by no others.

Even more "in short" or pointed is what was raised earlier by co-writer F. S. Flint and then affirmed by Pound: "As regarding rhythm: to compose in sequence of the musical phrase, not in sequence of a metronome." Sounds simple, yet much is involved. Since Pound stood against "chop[ping] your stuff into separate *iambs*," what would he have thought of chopping prose of little or no musical quality into lines of questionable or absent focus? That practice often seems to occur especially with the *facile* trend referred to in these pages, but evident at times in the *private-obscure* as well. Perhaps his comment of 100+ years ago fits today as well: "Freshmen in poetry are unfortunately not confined to a definite and recognizable classroom. They are 'all over the shop.' Is it any wonder 'the public is indifferent to poetry'?"

Glyn Maxwell, cited previously, elucidates Pound's view of musicality in poetry:

> . . . musical phrases can show infinite variety and still be supported by a regular structure of bars, 4/4 can turn to 3/8 or 9/16 or 2/4 and turn back again. These are called *time-signatures*—what's poetic meter but time-signature? The metronome does its boring job, but only a fool—literally an idiot—would write upon its strokes. The sound it makes doesn't make it to performance. The bars are silent, the notes sound. It seems to me some poets extrapolate Pound's critique of late Victorian pentameters—or the general Modernist argument against metrical form—to include, frankly, Shakespeare.

Maxwell, whose *On Poetry* makes a fine companion to Parini's *Why Poetry Matters*, has his own take on the shallowness or the utter falseness of the formalist vs. anti-formalist camps, or their ideologies:

> The fissure in writing poetry, the chasm between what I believe absolutely and doubt profoundly, is not between the "metrical" (say Frost) and the "musical" (say Pound)—which is a crude reduction of the work of both, albeit the kind of reduction writers in both camps have made ever since Robert and Ezra bickered on the pavements of Bloomsbury; the fissure is between a governing aesthetic *like either*—or having no governing aesthetic at all, which leaves you with nothing but your next thought, or your latest feeling. That's an impulse that waited ninety years to find its true literary form. It's called a blog.

What's wrong, one might ask, with writing poetry by "next thought"? Can't that be argued for as a "governing aesthetic"? Maxwell's later calling upon W. H. Auden helps explain the perceived problem in a way that fits the concerns of this preface: "Auden makes the supreme argument for poetic form in general, though he's making it here for meter in particular: 'Blessed be all rules that forbid automatic response, force us to have second thoughts, free from the fetters of Self.'" Yes, the problem is with too much self, with self-absorption, with lack of openness to greater possibilities, with lack of empathy for, or connection to, a greater audience, with limiting oneself to such an extent that one actually confines oneself, loses a greater freedom.

It's not just a matter of what we want to say, it's also *how can we best say it* in order to create meaning for or have an effect on an audience. Timing is very much a part of the "how," of form, of time-signatures. It's also not just the timing of the moment, but the timing of a continuum that we are all part of. Maxwell lays out the progression:

> This is all the difference is—between form and formlessness, between a governing aesthetic and nothing. You breathe the whiteness [that you write your black upon], you know lines have to end, you seek out words that fit the music. Your brain, freed from its dull day-job of serving up *the next thing you WOULD think because you're YOU*, delves deep into the vaults and libraries instead, the dusty sites and attics of all you've known or guessed or heard, sorting and rummaging for a word or phrase that not only *means* right but *sounds* right, *looks* right, *fits* right. Four ways of meaning. Up it comes. Now the poem is not only you, it's you and the language. It's not only you and today, it's you and time.

... writing that has broken clear of either the metrical or musical phrase and uses the word "free" for what it thinks it is now, just isn't up to that. . . . without those instruments that have grown out over centuries of speech to *form* the line, the stanza, the break, and the beats, all the evasions and allusions and insights you've got in your little quiver won't stop yourself doing what yourself likes doing.

Readers and listeners need more than the poet's "you" and his/her "liking" in the now. We need to make as much of the world and time as we can.

The "governing aesthetic" or "form" that Maxwell is focused on ultimately deals with musicality—in both "metrical" and "musical phrase" poetry. Even such extreme avant-garde types as Kenneth Goldsmith and his self-styled "uncreative writing" movement, who are generally focused on copying from practically any written material, either selectively or wholly, can argue about following a type of form or a governing aesthetic. But musicality? Vendler works at making a case on behalf of Jorie Graham for dispensing with music, with sound—with the fundamentally, scientifically, linguistically, musically, historically, humanly understood sense of rhythm:

The conventional view of the poetic line, as I have said, associates it with breath; and indeed, a great deal of theorizing about the material base of poetry, links it to the inspiration and suspiration of the single breath as its measure. The physiological regulation of breathing makes natural breaths roughly isometric—in, out; in, out. And isometric breathing is a likely basis for regular lines, orderly and successive ones. But the gaze has no such isometric rhythm: a gaze can be prolonged at will, held for inspection, meditated on, and periodically interrupted. It is the gaze, rather than the breath, that seems to be Graham's fundamental measure [in the "numbered line poems" in *The End of Beauty* and, by suggestion, beyond]. By this choice of the gaze over the breath, as a governing principle, Graham redefines utterance; and what utterance becomes is the tracking of the gaze, quantum-percept by quantum-percept, bundle by bundle, rhythm by rhythm. In Graham's poetry, a trust in the vagaries of the perceptual comes to replace the earlier poetry's trust in both the physiologically regulated order of breath and in a teleologically regulated order of truth.

"Redefines utterance"? Really? For whom exactly? "Rhythm by rhythm"? Since "vagaries" are involved, then a random or anti-rhythm rhythm? Do the lines actually get laid down by gazes that can be quite prolonged and also relatively short? Of course, there is that "quantum-percept by quantum-percept." Um. But what about *sound*? And what about *aud*ience? And purpose, beyond the attempted persuasion that any moment is all? And how many people really want to try to follow one person's pursuit of vagaries, or idiosyncratic embracing of random moments, which is its own teleology, or dysteleology? Keep breathing. It serves us well.

Such a focus on the gaze implies more attention on the visual, although some attempts are likely made to evoke other sense impressions in images presented. This relates to the greater focus on the visual sense since the advent of photography and its evolution into "moving pictures" and on into omnipresent screen presentations of all types. Susan Sontag in *On Photography* wrote of how "Industrial societies turn their citizens into image-junkies; it is the most irresistible form of mental pollution." Granted, her initial focus was more on still photography, but her overall concern was over a lack of full presentation, on a need for full disclosure, on a functioning over time, on how narration promotes greater understanding, on a knowledge that extends to the political, to the ethical, to wisdom. Would-be poems that are lacking in inherent language-musicality, in line-musicality, in voice-musicality, in a song quality that can be shared—such works move in the visual, limited, private, abstract direction.

Consider more about the visual and abstract, aside from the dominance of visual representation in the culture at large. Consider further, for example, the art critic John Ashbery and the abstract-expressionism-influenced poet Ashbery. Nick Laird, estimable poet, novelist, and critic himself, has done just that, referring in 2013 to the way Ashbery's "trajectory . . . mimics his coevals in the New York School of painters, like Kline or Arshile Gorky or Willem de Kooning, who began in figurative work and ended in abstractions." He quotes Ashbery: "the simultaneity of Cubism is something that has rubbed off on me, as well as the Abstract Expressionist idea that the work is a sort of record of its own coming-into-existence; it has an 'anti-referential sensuousness'. . ." Laird comments, ". . . maybe there is good reason for NOT SAYING: maybe we don't know what or how we are experiencing." In that case, what is being *shared with another or others*?

Laird's endorsement has a curious and honest reluctance: "It often seems so [the above] to me when I read Ashbery—though it's also true to say that I don't return often to his work, and I suspect it's because if you know a poem can go anywhere, all the terrains begin to seem alike, dreamscapes where anything can happen but nothing is real. . . . After all a dream, when you're in it, is completely consuming, even if it can't be retold—that is paraphrased—successfully." Certainly, one's own dream can be all-consuming.

But another's? Possibly, but generally very unlikely—to the point of the other person's dream being supremely off-putting (boring?) because of its supreme internality. We're back to a poetry of the highly private realm. The achievement of the influential Ashbery (and poets like him) may reach greatness at times, but, really, how many people will turn to or "return often to his work"?

To step back from the visual-abstract and return to the musical, there are those who will call their poetic efforts sonnets, odes, or, more generally, songs, but without offering anything that fits a sense of what a sonnet, an ode, or a song is. Perhaps such calling is metaphoric, ironic, or "redefining," as in "redefining utterance" above. Some more general or occasional musical claim may be made, with little or no musical element apparent, or audible. One might ask, so what? What does it matter? This: such wide naming or claiming may well result in a diminution of actual achievements musically, or even result in a loss of reality—please, no "alternative facts" in this area of life, in art.

Consider the importance of naming accurately, meaningfully, in what Andrew Delbanco has written about slavery and Frederick Douglass: "It was never an easy task to convey the brute reality of slavery to people for whom it was a faraway abstraction"—and, of course, it still is, although the film *12 Years a Slave* provided a fairly recent nudge. Delbanco then refers to Douglass's "exasperation" over an overly-free use of the word/idea "slavery": "It is common in this country to distinguish every bad thing by the name of slavery. Intemperance is a slavery; to be deprived of the right to vote is slavery, says one; to have to work hard is slavery, says another; and I do not know but that if we should let them go on, they would say that to eat when we are hungry, to walk when we desire to have exercise, or to minister to our necessities, or have necessities at all is slavery." Some substitutions and adaptations with respect to poetry might be enlightening, working within Delbanco's words: *It is never an easy task to convey the penetrating and moving reality of poetry . . .* , and then going on to fit into what Douglass offers: *It is common in this country to distinguish every concentrated piece of writing by the name of poetry . . .*

Continue on as you will or won't, the point should be clear. Just as there has been a long evolution of *story* or *narrative* accompanied by efforts at better, more distinguishing nomenclature, perhaps more effort could be made for what has evolved from *poem*, especially for works lacking in essential musical quality. We've had for a long time, for highly poetic paragraphs, the name "prose poem." For other poetic prose not presented in paragraphs, but chopped into lines, other gradations might be considered: *prosem, transpoem, dispoem, suppoesem, oppoesem,* or simply *posem,* take your pick. A creative—and fun—endeavor in itself? (*Dystopoeia?*)

More seriously, the musical element has been strongly focused on here because of its essential ability to bring poet and audience together—*essential* with respect to the emergence of humans, of human language with its sound systems, and of human songs/poems for their even further social, communal importance—and *essential* with respect to the continuation of all three. Neuroscientists and evolutionary psychologists alike continue to explore and discover how we are "hard-wired" for music, for song. The importance of musical quality in poetry was first significantly addressed in writing by Aristotle in *De Poetica* (*Poetics*), where in his focus on mimesis, long discussed and reconsidered over the centuries, he actually gives first attention to form—to rhythm, language, and harmony—before turning to objects and manner of imitation. The importance has played on, of course, for thousands of years.

We know how much easier it is to commit to memory musical poetry—and how it can then continue to sustain us from within. Catherine Robson, author of *Heart Beats: Everyday Life and the Memorized Poem*, has provided especially powerful examples: "In time of terrible, desperate straits when you've got absolutely nothing, all you've got is the contents of your head, and that is where a memorized poem can do incredible work. People have looked at this in Holocaust literature and gulag memoirs. There's no gulag memoir without someone saying, 'Thank goodness I've got Pushkin.'" Or in a simpler and more general regard, she offers, ". . . it's good to have this poem inside you . . . it's something you can think about. It's like this little internal gymnasium, that you can go and play in it." "Think about," yes, but "play" also. The musical sounds themselves play; notes and harmony resonate more.

The Poetry Foundation has widely put forth, "As the philosopher Richard Rorty observed . . . in an essay for *Poetry*, 'individual men and women are more fully human when their memories are amply stocked with verses,'" and with good reason. The less private, the more musical, the more likely the "stocking." Above all, the more connected we are, and so the "more fully human."

Bob Dylan won the Nobel Prize in Literature for 2016 "for having created new poetic expressions within the great American song tradition." Was the reference to song an intended or unintended, conscious or unconscious, comment on the lack of musical quality in so much of contemporary poetry—and on the need for more of it?

Long before Dylan, Duke Ellington and Irving Mills wrote,

It don't mean a thing
If it ain't got that swing

. . . .

All you got to do is sing

. . . .

It makes no difference
If it's sweet or hot
Just give that rhythm
Everything you got

Oh, it don't mean a thing
If it ain't got that swing

Those lyrics didn't win any Nobel Prize, nor should they have, of course, but they may capture an essential truth. It's called "swing," all right, not just by musicians but even by oarsmen in crew. Michael J. Socolow has written of swing in crew as "a metaphysical feeling of transcendence." He quotes from Mihaly Csikszentmihalyi's *Flow: The Psychology of Optional Experience*, noting the closeness of "flow" to "swing": "Flow begins when one is 'completely involved in an activity for its own sake. The ego falls away. Time flies. Every action, movement, and thought follows inevitably from the previous one, like playing jazz.'" Socolow adds that the experience of swing can't be forced or obsessed over: "[It], in this sense, is closely related to Zen, or existential feelings bridging the ephemeral and the enduring." No forcing or obsessing over, no expecting or demanding transcendence, no requiring of a grand vision or of salvation or of solving huge sociopolitical problems or of being a prophet (cf.

Lerner, Chen, Edmundson, et al.). The key: *an experience without ego, a supreme connecting.* People who have no singing ability can be transported when they join their voices in a chorus, formally or informally—as was the case when a flash mob appeared in Placa de Sant Roc in Barcelona some years ago, the passersby stopping to raise their voices to Beethoven's "Ode to Joy," if they could, or at the very least to give way to their spirits' being raised. All of it occurring in a still point of time, or in a still point of the turning universe. Transported, indeed.

With poetry, the transcendence can and does occur when a reader-listener joins the voice-song of a poet and participates in—*completes*—the creation, or the re-creation of life, word by word and note by note. A timeless moment, but one that the reader-listener can revisit, and will want to revisit, time and again.

In the end, this preface has been political. But it's not the politics of what sociopolitical issues to address in poetry. These pages, after all, have not been about subject matter, about what to write about, other than *not* to make the poet too much the subject—the personal that becomes too personal, that offers little or no connection to readers/listeners, that becomes, in effect, "private, no admittance." Or that requires select club membership. The politics herein has been that which is the ultimate concern—the self in relation to others—especially "the other" who *seems* so different, so inferior, as to be deserving of dismissal or discrimination against. It has been the politics of how the self is to *live with those others,* including how to *write poetry that can connect with them.* We have had George Orwell's "Politics and the English Language." Perhaps, in its own way, this essay is "Politics and Poetic Language" or simply "Politics and Poetry."

Undemocratic governments, societies, and social groups, big and small, are about some people setting themselves above, usually far above, others. People in general are obviously not all the same. There are varying qualities or attributes, strengths and weaknesses, if you will. But *equality* is not the same as, does not equal, *sameness*. "If my cup won't hold but a pint, and yours holds a quart, wouldn't you be mean not to let me have my little half-measure full?" (Sojourner Truth, "Ain't I a Woman?"). *The issue* is about equal rights as human beings, about treating others fairly, equally, humanely, be it in politics or in poetry.

I'm aware that I may be misunderstood in referring to something of a malaise in American poetry. Old Jimmy Carter eventually came to grief over his "Malaise in America" speech (actual title "Crisis of Confidence"), a view very soon rejected in favor of Reagan's "Morning in America." So, a malaise in *all* of our poetry, really? (No, of course not.) *Nothing* good going on? (No, there's a lot of good.) And who the hell do I think I am, setting myself up in judgment this way? (A very small gadfly, nothing more.) Surely, I have tried to be careful about generalizations, hoping to avoid overgeneralizing. At the same time, I have also tried to identify strong trends that I believe are of concern, and I have tried to indicate larger social, cultural, and, yes, political connections. The extreme form of focusing on oneself, of being self-absorbed, short of pathology, is commonly referred to as narcissism, and the current president is widely seen, even by some supporters and abettors, as a particular, highly prominent case of narcissism. The question has become whether he will represent, or already does represent, a "new norm." Perhaps, instead, he is a culmination, the end of a long-evolved, or long-devolved (from individualism over equality) norm for the country as a whole, not just politically, economically, and socially but also culturally. "Culturally," of course, includes poetry.

Actually, instead of "short of pathology," matters of pathology in the social scene have, in fact, recently been addressed by clinically trained social/cultural critics. Joel and Ian Gold have written about how culture has a role in the development of psychopathology. Martha Stout has addressed our society's "run-amok individualism" and how "It seems likely that, in the United States especially, any genetic predisposition to sociopathy will be nurtured and shaped by a single-mindedly competitive and individualistic culture."

But this preface has already raised what is ultimately of concern, what is ultimately at stake—nothing less than the survival of democracy and, far greater yet, the survival of life itself on Earth. Remember how the Doomsday Clock was at two-and-a-half minutes to midnight as of January 2017? What has followed? Two years later, the Science and Security Board of the *Bulletin of the Atomic Scientists* reset the clock to two minutes to midnight, the closest it had been since 1953 and the advent of the hydrogen bomb. Others, be it Daniel Ellsberg or *The Nation* magazine, have powerfully argued that the danger is even greater than that. Or as the chair of the Board stated in 2019, "We're playing Russian roulette with humanity." The odds worsened further per the *Bulletin* for January 2020, "It Is 100 Seconds to Midnight." As Editor John Mecklin reaffirmed, "The Clock has become a universally recognized indicator of the world's vulnerability to catastrophe from nuclear weapons, climate change, and new technologies emerging in other domains." The Covid-19 pandemic, closely linked to climate change, emerged worldwide after January 2020. A further running out of time?

Culturally, beyond the arts in general, poetry in particular can, instead of just going along, try to counteract our dangerous direction by seeking to engage more people, by being more democratic itself, by being more inclusive with respect to audience. Strength for the effort may be gained from so many sources, including the following range of voices.

From William Dalrymple on "The Renaissance of the Sultans," particularly Ibrahim Adil Shah II of the kingdom of Bijapur, in the Deccan sultanates of India ca. 1600:

> . . . Ibrahim presided over a freethinking court in which art was a defining passion. . . . In his poems he dwells on its ability to bring people together . . . *nauras* became the central theme of Ibrahim's reign; the word expresses the binding aesthetic force that he hoped would hold the diverse subjects and religions of his empire together. . . . Through music and art, he believed that his people could learn to look at others with mutual understanding: "They speak different languages, / But they feel the same thing: / The Turk and the Brahmin."

From Goethe, *Wilhelm Meister's Apprenticeship*:

> . . . esteem[ing] . . . all that testified or forwarded the worth and unity of human nature; . . . shun[ning] and condemn[ing] nothing else so heartily as individual pretension and narrow exclusiveness.

From Seamus Heaney:

> Poetry, let us say, whether it belongs to an old political dispensation or aspires to express a new one, has to be a working model of inclusiveness.

From Americana singer-songwriter Bill Staines:

All God's creatures got a place in the choir,
Some sing low and some sing higher,
Some sing out loud on a telephone wire,
Some just clap their hands, or paws, or anything they've got now.

From Jay Parini:

Most crucially, perhaps, poetry restores the culture to itself: mirroring what it finds there already but also sensing and embodying the higher purposes and buried ideals of that culture, granting access to hidden sources of power.

From Walt Whitman:

The proof of a poet is that his country absorbs him as affectionately as he has absorbed it.

Pace any who may feel apart.

For all, simply *pacem*.

Coming to Light,
An Advent Progress

A man (Voice One) in winter hat and coat, plus a muffler covering half his face, makes his way from the back of the theater up the center aisle, beating his arms across his chest as if still trying to ward off the cold, and steps directly onto the stage. He passes between a small red sofa fronted by a coffee table (bearing a tiny Christmas tree) immediately before him and, to the left, a café-style table with two chairs, and continues on to a hat and coat tree in the back of the room. He removes his hat, coat, and muffler with his back to the audience. When he turns and faces forward, people can see that he's wearing a white mask, which is the last thing he removes and then hangs up in such a way that it, too, faces everyone. He returns to the front, passing between the right end of the sofa and a short bar with two stools further to the right, and arrives back before the coffee table. Along the way, he gestures toward the mask and begins—

Mummery

I placed a mime in Massachusetts,
In wintry night, and let him be.
I marked a poem in some rime,
He watched, then played it silently—
Just so could Pierrot be muse.

The black sky fell in snow-white whimsy,
A match for Pierrot and me:
Composedly, in kind and two,
We traced the song for all to see
In snow and air and *comme-ci* rhythm.

Come join our mummers-retinue,
We welcome nimble minds and limbs,
There's no admission price or fee,
No passing muster, rungs to climb—
You here? We're glad *you* made it, too.

Starting with "Come join our mummers-retinue," another man (Voice Five) and a woman (Voice Six), also in winter outerwear, slowly enter from the left, and two other women (Voices Two and Three) and one other man (Voice Four), wiping his hands with a handkerchief, enter from the right as from rest rooms. All five of these newcomers look in a welcoming way to the audience, and at the conclusion of One's invitation, they complete their momentary business, Five and Six hanging their hats and coats in back and taking seats at the café table, Two sitting on the right side of the sofa, and Three and Four on the two stools. At the end of One's offering, the lights dim briefly, then come back up.

Voice Two: Pierrot—qu'est que c'est *(pointing backwards at the mask)*? *(When One gestures for her to hold forth, she rises and steps forward, pointing toward the audience—)* Que de monde! *(Then, as One retires to sit on the left of the sofa, she offers—)*

Snow Woman

Snow Woman admits of no
Formation, lying cold and still
Upon the hardened bed of earth.

Snowmen, by course, promptly roll out,
All primped, patted, and bally-hooed—
But she just lies there waiting, stiffening,

Pure white *un*-folded. No one perceives
Her flat undulations across
Vacant fields and yards, the drift

To crevice, the blue veins running
Under ice, the greater rotation
Of all—unless moved to *conceive*,

To bear witness to what will be.
Living in the moment, who can tell time,
Or reveal secret identity?

The lights again dim briefly, then come back up.

As Two resumes her seat, **Voice Three** *nods approval and begins address-ing Two and the other "mummers," then expands to all present.*

Word

Word went out on Thanksgiving that the crescent
Moon, Venus, and Jupiter would converge,
Form a bright triangle in the southwestern
Sky. Few noticed, paid heed, with all the words
That just come and go all the time beyond
Much meaning or caring or owning to.
Word was the light was bright, indeed—a trinity
A finger's width apart, hand held out so.
Word came of a second chance, Christmas now,
Of our brightest star at its closest, light
In the east at sunset so close—reach out,
Word was, so that you could almost touch it!
Missed again? The moon continues in flight,
Yet drifts down, word has it, as dark made light.

As after every poem, the lights dim briefly, then come back up.

Voice Four bounces off his stool and takes center stage behind the sofa, playing in part to the three women on stage as well as to his recreated "Shadow Lake," offering the following with a hint of rap style—

Three Silly Maidens

Three, not five, silly maids *not* on the make,
Gamboling across crusted Shadow Lake
(With the black, not red, spot for safety's sake),
Toward unseen, peripheral me—brake, brake!

Freeze—what? Sidelong and straight-on looks—what, what?
They stand close, under roseate sky, cut
Against a backdrop of silver-white, nut
Brown solid shapes, grace in state, near abutting.

I shut my motor so as not to scare—
Stay, carry on while I stop, let me stare at
Sturdy, robust, anti-Bambi you, daring
Me to move. You will go untouched where

I can't. But maybe share with my own kind?
I try to wave others down—none of mind
To join this flailing figure, none to find
A rare transient beauty. Golden hind?

O come now! One silver Volvo does slow,
So I risk opening my door to show, to
Love as only humans can. But the does
Won't have it, exiting left, bounding over

Fallen branches, with a last hover, tail
With a last flip up, white, pointed, impaling
Me on the spot, stirring a surge of maleness,
An impossible yearning, complete failure.

I think to say a last word: did you see?—
But the Volvo pulls out, away, can't be
Lingering or bothered. There is no we,
The maidens gone, the scene empty, save me.

Lights dim, come up.

__Voice Five__ rises and gestures some sympathy to Four before crossing to the tiny Christmas tree on the coffee table and "interacting" with it, and with all present—

Web

The *real* ordeal of ornamenting
    the tree begins, always
adding, never subtracting, minus
    the fallen beyond raising,

but even those are kept, lamented
    over, picked up, put down
year to year, the invested meaning
    compounded, interest drawn.

"Dad's angel," tiny, golden, with blood-
    red, nine-petaled, back halo
(six parts still there) is set aside
    just for me, with my "yellow

bird" next to her, tinier still,
    red-chested, silent-songed
canary of peace. Well, it's well
    for me to string along,

feel a part of family, close up;
    some old even seem new:
six-pointed red star, plastic-cheap,
    white baby Jesus glued

in the middle, reaching . . . okay,
     next to angel and bird
you go. Just so. Then Allie takes
     her turn to place our star

on high in all its satin-puff
     glory, where just before
fearful dad had reached and combed off
     a web of angel's hair.

Lights dim, come up.

Voice Six emits a little grunt and cocks her head at Five's quasi-complaint, then responds to him and to all present, giving the words "Holyoke" and "fixed" special emphasis.

Holyoke

The Holyoke of John DiNapoli and
Eddie Morales is forever fixed:
Police officer and drug dealer, Anglo
And Hispanic, killed and killer, lives crossed.
Close by, "locked down" inside Peck Middle School,
I have the eighty-plus students of 8B
Listening still on the cold, hard linoleum
To stooled peers theatre-adapting Grace Paley's
"The Loudest Voice": my "Baby Jesus kept
His head. We all kept our heads," her "I had
Prayed for everybody." How many ripped
Johns, Eddies, lives, souls? How many're saved?
Outside, the "Massive Manhunt," winter chill,
And, absent, Jessenia having her child.

Lights dim, come up.

One, rising from the sofa, is compelled to ask Six about what she has just shared—

Voice One: Jessenia?
Voice Six: Yes.
Voice One: How old?
Voice Six: Fourteen.
Voice One: What . . . ?

Unable to go further, **One** *looks around vacantly, then, recovering some presence of mind, starts patting his different pockets, searching. He soon finds in his left inside breast pocket what he has been looking for: of all things, a pomegranate. This is the best he can offer to everyone, by the end placing the fruit next to the Christmas tree on the coffee table—*

Pome, Poem

What to make of a pomegranate? Red
Yet yellow, round yet planed, Sidon – Granada,
Fruit – grenade, divine – heathen, fertile – dead,
Seeding to the Sun, buried unto Hades?

What of the seeds: suck dry and spit, or eat?
Eat like a Persephone, bound to death?
Bleed like an Adonis and flower at
The tears of Venus? Or behold the birth

Of Christ and know new life, saving death, Life
Evermore? Stores of despair, yet of hope
Overarching, soothing still—but belief?
The pomegranate becomes Chinese apple.

So pome the fruit!—cut without thought through hide—
Tear into recessed chambers—dig down nails
Through white, wafer-thin membranes—sink—embed
Lips, teeth, and tongue into just-bursting cells—

Stain fingertips, mouth, face, soul, what have you.
Nothing to chance. Poem the fruit, make, do.

Lights dim, come up.

Three responds by leaving her stool to move to the right end of the sofa and share what she has "made of" the house sparrow.

Voice Three: Yes, what to make of.

The House Sparrow

The house sparrow nests behind the green shutters
Beside our bedroom window, fall to winter on
It is October-brown, November-gray, December-white
It rustles, flutters, throbs, palpitates, quivers
And settles back against the near wall
It peers in as we peer out; we are true peers
It will, unscreened, peck up the dead summer flies on the sill
It will, as well, pass in its mites to share with us
It will not, unbid, fall any time soon, perched between
Where we are and what will be
It is *passer domesticus*, it is generally unwanted
It has no discernible spirit, it just acts like one
It is just

Lights dim, come up.

Voice Four stands in turn, and as he offers the following, Three "sits" on the sofa arm in response to line five, and at the end "returns" to her stool next to him.

Winter Wake

I stand and watch my wife roll up from bed,
The white sheet foaming down her sides in ripples
As she breaks free, floats up, and shakes her head
In gentle swells above the fathoms deep.

She sits bed edge and bears my joy of her,
My Pisces—porpoise!—so-called for her full-
Figured, sleek, streaming, buoyant grace, for sure.
But she doubts me, my irony. That's all.

She trails on, off into the day, away
From metaphors that can't course straight, or else
Be real. I follow as I must, and make
My money, earn more, get spent, keep the daily

Faith, till her return, stirring me again.
Then night, and sleep, and wait the morning wonder.

Lights dim, come up.

Voice Six hasn't quite moved on as One had hoped to lead the group to do; some note of death and "wonder" in Four's poem causes her to shift uncomfortably on her chair and to interject, "God," the start of her shared musing—

He Laughed, Hard

God, how he cried coming into this world,
Old man's hand slapping his backside hard, this
Son of woman alone in fear and wisdom—
The cutting of the cord, the dark, the cold.
Learning of wood and nails, a carpenter,
Bearing the hard Roman demand for crosses,
This son, when twelve, wandered away, stayed past
His time in the temple, yet claimed no tears.
Another wandering off, as a man,
On a desert precipice, a hard tempting
Of self, of God; then again to the temple—
Raging! Final cry of being abandoned.
Above all, for all our sorrows, Kristine,
He laughed, hard, this divine comedian.

Lights dim, come up.

Voice Two goes to Six, offering for her and for all present the following—

Malus Domestica

A vernal-white, virginal sallying forth,
An even downright dallying, before blue
Eyed gazing, or gray or brown looks, ensue;
A faint, initial blush in turn, from north
To south exposed, past any holding back—
Rosaceous blooming, red-cored, with firm arms
And full bosom, a greening growth to charm,
Our Lady Apple so appears, in fact.
The air gives way to whisper, buzz—heard, seen,
Known, borne as fruit. Then fall must come: skin shrivels,
Limbs thin out, chest sinks in, and spirit's shriven—
Still, green-red holds till dark's made light, stead Queen.
He comes to rest, now quiet, mourning dove,
As she remains, ever, in truth, so lovely.

Lights dim, come up.

Voice Five has his own, different, yet related response to Six, seated at the café table next to her, recalling a family lunch at a Chinese restaurant—

Counting

Chicken with mixed vegetables,
Chicken in garlic sauce,
Two luncheon specials for four,
With two extra soups, won ton,
And an endless supply of fried won tons
On demand, constant.

Saving diversion:
Five on the tenth boy,
With four to go to the twenty-fifth,
With a secret to share,
Two white hands pulling,
Two pink lips pushing,
Flesh and spirit one, transporting—
Let's get Mom a nightgown
For Christmas!
(Right on the money,
Done!)
Looks around of pleased wonder,
More soggy won tons,
More snappy "One!" ones—
Let's get Mom some slippers
For Christmas!

(Right on the money again,
Done, done!)
The angelic host isn't done,
Beats all—
Let's get Allie a lit-tle, lit-tle, lit-tle
Barbie!
(Good enough,
Bingo!)
Eight-and-three-quarters girl
Gives the commentary—
This family is really some-
Thing when it's together.

Then the wait,
Waiting, waiting, waiting
On the waiter,
On the fortune
Cookies, past won tons.
Finally,
Ev's
"You will be lucky and
Overcome many hardships."

On comes baby Jesus,
Right on the money,
Done.

Lights dim, come up.

Picking up on some apprehension in Five, and in the oth
Four *comes forward, addressing himself at first to Five, bu*
mediately to everyone. The thought of a singled-out "everyon
five causes Three to come up behind Four and give him a sm
back of his shoulder. His response in lines six to nine is met u
stomp from her. When he persists to the end, she decides t
arms and a laser stare will suffice.

N

You must be scared—I am the Winter Monster.
But I'm no whistling wind outside your window,
Just a *whisp* beside your bed—let me in,
Let me slip between your sheets, blue-white shins
Inching toward your sleepy calves, fleshy, pink.
I'm no abominable snowman to shun,
Merely arctic monkey bars you can swing on;
A long metal slide, smooth, slippery, shiny;
Whole steely playground—press your lips just once.
An icicle of intercontinental
Ballistic missile measure? My mis*sion*
Is only heat-seeking, your tropic zone
My only target—a warm nestling in.
You mustn't be scared—I am the Winter Monster.

Lights dim, come up.

December Romance

December—not April cruelest, nor June
In moon—must be the most romantic month,
Why else make men of snow, or gods of men,
Or turn the world virgin-white, life in death?

At dusk, a chickadee, cold-ruffed, calls out
For light, for *PHOE-be*, not because he's fool-
Hardy, in touch with nothing there, but cut
From deep within, by force unnameable.

Up close, our frosted windows filigree
With silvery stems and baby's breath, marking
Our turn of mind from ice to what we see
In the glaze, and search on for through the dark.

We feel the creeping cold, approaching death,
Yet know a surging warmth, a lasting breath.

Lights dim, come up.

Voice Six rises and steps toward Three, stopping at the left edge of the sofa—

At Long Last

I notice, tend, the black and white of five
AM, top of our stairs, out our back window,
From hip roof down to back slope up: no living
Thing, nothing moving, only glossy moon glow—

Like winter starlings gathered, like the one
Released from our center chimney last year:
Flue down, it flew out, hit our picture window,
Then waddled grimly about, till, head snared,

It was made off—
                          like my mother at ending
Time, white-skinned, darkness growing, final noting:
Her mouth agape, face beaked, spiritus flown—

Like us: we, too, at long last, will be nothing.

Lights dim, come up.

Voice Two has an "answer" for Six and Three as she comes forward from the sofa to the front and they cross back to their seats—

Second Coming, Bethlehem and Baghdad
(In Case You Missed It, or Set It Aside)

Joe and Mare are going to Bethlehem,
Reconciled to her having their first child;
She got pregnant somehow, and he's just numb
About it. Abortion? No. God has willed.

Actually, Mare's sick about it all,
Joe acts like an old man since he came home,
Pain in his joints, burning discharge . . .

                                           Metallic
Ribbon-magnets on cars and trucks go humming

By: "God Bless America," "Support Our Troops,"
"United We Stand"—so they read again
And again, so Mare tries to pick Joe up
Again and again, but she knows they're alone

Now. Their present, their future, only theirs.
Joe won't talk about the past, about Baghdad,
About Abu Ghraib—well, he wasn't near
That crap or any abuses you see fagged

On TV. Responsibility lies
With the "rogue few." But YOU just try to deal
With the Baathists, insurgents, terrorists—
War is war. Joe said that much. War is hell

22

Also. The image of that one prisoner,
Though, still flashes in Mare's mind: the dog strains
Toward him, the guy's buck naked, but his fingers
Are locked behind his head with his arms down

Along his neck. Why? He would sacrifice
His genitals to save his life. What if
That were Joe? Or maybe Joe's time to lose
Is here, now? Oh, God, she's got to put off

These thoughts! Please, it's Christmas Eve, time for hope—
Joe had to be safe, he'd been safe inside
His Abrams tank, he's even got a tape
Of them rolling into downtown "Saddam-land,"

The main drag, unfired upon, and then blasting
The Ministry of Planning, the DU
Shells just pulverizing the concrete as
If it were cake frosting. All that dust. Phew.

But the DU in the dust? Did Joe breathe
Any of that in? And why the delays
In checking him out? No holding her breath
Waiting, it's her husband and it's her baby,

So she called some veterans' group, some "Resource
Center," to find out about Gulf War Syndrome,
Alpha radiation, cancer, birth defects.
Joe doesn't know her fears. She protects him.

Is that fear that churns in her gut, her womb?
Does she bear a half-life of four-and-a-half

Billion years? She feels that old. Her child's time
Is coming. Wintering blackbirds wheel above . . .

Mare feels all, nothing, now—she sees Jesús,
Her baby who'll never see, his gaze blank,
Who'll go unpitied by the pitiless,
Those in power and money and sin so drunk—

And she knows without saying that her son
Has a brother, some Mohammed, in Iraq,
Also blighted, or leukemic and soon
To die—knows, too, that their families are locked

Together in pain and despair and love.
No "nucular" sickness can overcome
Their shared humanity and essential life.
They will endure on earth, and for all time.

Lights dim, come up.

*Voice Five breaks the string of female voices, drifting from his café table
seat to the front left corner—*

Mattering

Told my teen daughter I wanted to kill
Santa Claus for Christmas. Couldn't escape
Her horror, disgust—explain I meant well!
Couldn't pass off purging from us US types

The Fat Guy, the Great American Excess,
X-Mass Consumption, Unchecked Capitalism,
World-Wasting Greed. Wished for Saint Nicholas
The original, fourth-century bishop

Of Myra, secret provider of dowries
For three impoverished daughters, otherwise
Slaves; restorer of three youngsters whose bodies
Had been cut up and pickled in brine—what's

A Coca-Cola Claus, thousands of selling
Santas, to that? Irving, Moore, Nast, and Coke
Led the Americanization, all
Easily seen. But mattering? We make

It go. Willingly. Willfully. Hearts leading
Us on. We Kris Kringles. We *Christ-Kindlein.*

Lights dim, come up.

*The serious turns have affected **Voice Four**. He leaves his seat and moves to the front right corner, opposite to Five. He points to the back of the theater as if standing in his classroom—*

Pinwheel

In the back of my classroom stands Blake's car
Bearing Dante's blest *Beatrice*;
In martial middle, ranked desks, each
Packing a lexicon in undercarriage;
On one book's pressed pages, surprise!—a raised
Nazi swastika.

Find the kid who did it, turn him in to turn
Him out? Or claim "a teaching moment,"
Redeem the inditer, if woe
Like that might ever be removed, might ever
Cease being banal? Maybe one should give
Credit—extra—for burning

Hate not on synagogue wall or lav stall,
But on language itself, on thought,
A ready reference, a wrought
Consciousness, edginess? Perhaps one must
Pass on the sinner instead, deal with just
The sin, that is, in all

Literalness—save at least time and trouble,
Change what can be changed, blacken out
The offense with more ink (no doubt

A "cover-up," but what the hell)? Would "Wite-
Out" be better? Or the ultimate hit,
Scissor snipping, eh, bubba?

We mouth each day, ". . . with liberty and justice
For all," and study Douglass, Twain,
Truth, Addams, Joseph, Peltier, Tan,
Cisneros, King, and on, but to what end?
The Indian benediction is bent
Backwards, blessing made curse,

Love made hate, again and again, a wheeling
Known all too well. Wheel, whorl, Blake-Dante
Vortex, spirit-world spinning on,
Esti, asti, ist, is . . . This then: add four
More arms, close the figure, window it. More
Pinwheel, if you will. Still.

Lights dim, come up.

Voice One looks to four, stirs, and opens his mouth as if to console, but no words come forth. His gaze shifts back, only to turn downward. Then, with considerable effort, he wills himself to break the momentary, heavy silence, rising from the sofa and stepping forward. He redirects, pointing to the ceiling—

Midwest Dogma, No Doubt

My dog's roof-roofing on the roof
How he got there, I do not know
He doesn't act above it all
No role reversal, dog to god
Sincere, authentic, unironic
And not the least upset, or joyful
No raising of the roof, or roof beam
He's just his own barbaric yawp
So all that's left to deal with now
Is how, good grief, to get him down
It's rough, no doubt. But not that rough.

Lights dim, come up.

As One sits again on the sofa, Four drifts back toward his stool, and **Voice Three** *crosses to stand behind One, at a certain point resting her hands on his shoulders, in mutual comfort. She ties her ending with "and that's enough" to One's preceding "But not that rough"—*

Winter Dreams

Friday, after midnight, I took nine holly
Leaves, tied them up in nine pagan knots, put
Them in a white, clean cloth under my pillow,
And set to make my ghostly dreams aright:
Saturnalia dispelled the saturnine;
Lightning, poisons, spirits, and wild beasts held
Off; the Holly King found his Ivy Queen;
And pink blossoms of spring returned, revealed
The lily-white inner core giving birth
To wondrous blood-red berries, mother-son
Love that casts off wintry dark, gloom, and death,
Turning gall to sweetness, thorns to a crown.
Dreams end, memories haunt on. At winter's end, though,
Robins gorge on the berries, and that's enough.

Lights dim, come up.

Voice Five returns to his chair to address Three and One at first, and then opens up his continuing struggle to all—

In Place

Can you will faith, can you will feeling? If
Not, then what—put yourself in place and hope?
The ladybug passing the upper left
Of the bathroom cabinet mirror stops—
At my stare, I think. Maybe at my breath.
We're close, my examination, her look:
Placid, rounded back, just above a pith
Of flat, furious skeleton—head, legs, trunk
Still a moment, fearing an enemy?
She's not lovely, I'm not friendly, her kind
An infestation, my place a wintry
Haven for these beetles who can bite, sting,
Hurt somehow, I'm told. A mass huddled in
The high corner, six shells grouped on the floor
Near the wastebasket. Coming to an end,
She must not see herself on the glass, or
Know anything. Then again, moving as bid,
She sprouts wings and flies off, back of my head.

Lights dim, come up.

Voice One begins his reply from the sofa, but he follows his words of re-enactment to go, in line eight, "on his knees"—

With E. M. Forster in Kerala, "God's Own Country"

St. Anthony's lies outside Wayanad
Wildlife Sanctuary, lights strung across
A spare, fronting tree and the church façade.
Godfrey had offered midday welcome, tossed
Off thirty-five as the number of families
In the parish; now it's ten o'clock mass
On Christmas Eve as this ghost of a man
Comes, finds a place, and goes down on his knees
On the wine-red floor. Pain closing, he seeks
Otherness as a big brown moth goes flitting
Up and back, fluorescence beckoning. Christ
Crucified, now in Malayalam*, looks out
At all alone, hands, feet, even knees bleeding;
Then, bread bit melting away, the moth settles.

*Pronounced *mah-LAHL-um*

Lights dim, come up.

Bear All, One

How did you come to be, such a poor child,
Conceived and later left to die alone?
But ever and anon we're forced to yield to
Your memory, what is, and will be done.
Try as we might, we can feel you at breast,
Faint yet steady breath seeking, seeking still,
Scarred hands hard at rest across your back, soft
Comfort against the dark and spirit frail.
Trod earth, rotted straw, dung, urine, and sweat
Coil with life's liquid, roil with it, fecund,
The flesh and blood of the moment shared, shed,
Leaving us with nothing but time to cut.
So we bear your life and death, bear all, one,
Lose time after time, eternity win.

Lights dim, come up.

Close as she is, **Voice Three** *adds quietly . . .*

Shivered

In Hermon barn

Harness bells
Rust encrusted
Leather creased
   And cracked

Slip their rung
Streak the dark
And jangle once
   A crown

To shivered hay

Brrr . . . amen.

Lights dim, come up.

Epistle on Cosmology

At sixteen, I stood before and confronted
Our father about . . . knowing God. Or not
Knowing. His reply: faith, alone. No further
Word. I could not believe, absent the force
Of argument. Later, I quit on math
(Mr. Luz offered no light); I went with

Reading alone: "English," "Humanities,"
Really everything. On the books, my official
Position now: English. Truly, it's fishing
In all waters: religion, science, God,
No God, Maybe. I hold just this: we've got
To have facts *and* feelings. We need the ties.

Yale astronomer van Dokkum has gazed
Into elliptical galaxies, pricks
Of light drifting into view like snow crystals
That never touch (a far-off firn), and guessed,
With Harvard astrophysicist (and bookend)
Conroy, three hundred sextillion sum stars,

Three times what scientists had calculated
(Assuming spans like our Milky Way spiral),
Thus a less orderly cosmos, unsettling
To many. For van Dokkum, all the sizes

Typecast as red dwarfs become "a big pain,"
But for Conroy the game begins—"It's fun

Thinking about these large numbers," like how
The stars equal all the cells in us humans
On Earth, or how they're like the seemingly
Limitless variety of shapes found
Of snowflakes—three hundred sextillion? You
Never know for sure. Each and every

One unique like six-appendaged *Copito
De Nieve*? Ah, the sex of six, of science,
Of cutting, splitting, calculating, just so.
So, Christmas Eve, I slipped out with red vino
In one hand, microscope in other, to find
The Star of David descend, with blood ester.

Lights dim, come up.

Caught

I was sweeping snow off our porch when caught
By something moving up along the wall
Beneath our kitchen window—what? a wobbling,
Shaken brown spider still alive in all
The wet chill from winter's first storm, its sleep,
Or death doze, broken by my human action.
But no, it was the wind alone that whipped
Some last, shredded web and, with it, attached,
An egg sac. What design was this? I wanted
To know. Inspection showed a backside hole,
But also a long insect limb that ran
Along the bag, a moth's or mother's, who
Could tell? I caught the fragile sac by touch
Alone, with plans to magnify, but then—
It filled my eyes, wafting me off the porch
Like the moon rising above snow and wind—
Then gone. Still, there behind the window, vased,
A pine branch in water, its own plain grace.

Lights dim, come up.

Voice Six takes Five by the hand to go stand together in the left-front, in balance with One and Two, with an open space between the two pairs—

Transfigure

Our Norfolk pines become three kings this time
Of year, ceiling-reaching, green-robed, arms flowing
Outward, offering . . . mere majesty, it seems,
Too weak to make more show of love, bear tokens.
We'll chop, bring in, prop up some pine, the thing
To do, yet maybe sense the way it shapes,
The way it points, the way it lets us hang
New apple and wafer forms, all our hopes.
We'll water it until it dies, then take
It out to dry, decay, and decompose
In our burial gully beside the Tabor
Hill of oaks, now skeletal, ghostly, whose
Brown leaves drape the golgotha granite base—
Until the weeping larch springs green, in grace.

Lights dim, come up.

Three crosses to take Four by the hand and proceed together to fill the space between the other two pairs. But it is **Voice Four** *who concludes—*

Mary Among Us

How many of us men are Zechari'ahs,
Who, doubting the angels that come among us,
Are struck dumb by mere appearance of fire,
Whorl of incense—full of fear, yet unsprung?

Compare Elizabeth, reproach of men,
Hiding herself, her deepest faith, until
A kinswoman, a Mary, appears, rends
The veils of silence, magnifies what will.

O, give credit to the just Josephs who
At least abide the angels of their own
Dreams, and to the Zechari'ahs who, too,
Come around once the facts are born out, known.

They loose their tongues, exceeded only by
The keepers of the flocks by night, who require
Special effects not to be missed by eye
Or ear, this or any time-rime, full choir

Of tenor, baritone, bass, swelling high,
Putting on a grand show themselves, just started
—Soon gone. It's left to Mary to keep nigh
All these things, pondering them in her heart.

For she alone holds the moment, the passing
Of spirit to flesh, new and everlasting.

All exit. Lights go down, except—

One small light, at the back of the stage, rests upon the white mask.

Green

Lead

The lilies of the valley around our house
So small, so white, so delicate
Like little bells that ring so softly
I could not hear them
If only I could!
Me picking some for my mom
Her putting them in water
In my favorite peanut butter glass
The one with the red and yellow
And blue balloons floating up and up
And the black string
Dangling
Down

Fishing

The swaying of the rowboat on the lake
The water under us feeling like a giant pillow
The sunfish looking like a child
The big-mouth bass smacking its Coke-bottle lips
The "hornpout" looking black-mustached, evil-ugly, dangerous
The hard pulling of life at the other end of the line
My father yelling, "Don't let him go under the boat!"
The sudden snapping of the line
My chest going all empty
My wonder
That fish

Kid Lit

at the circus
    everybody loves the clowns
but i fear the frowns
    of the clowns

mike the ringmaster
    crackshiswhiP
at ADAM THE STRONGMAn
    and eveN her fat ladyship

the expectant crown is riveted
    to the iron environs
of the lion tamer's devouring
    of his lions

and my mother
      s   s
         w   g
           i   n
through the s p o t l i g h t s
    in black tights

at the circus
    everybody loves the clownings
(but i fear the frownings)
    of the clown

Just Like

Hair duck-tailed, pants pegged, white socks stuffed
In black engineer boots, he gave the "Go!"—
Side-skipped back, a nearly off-balance Nureyev,
Patted the elliptical missile cocked by his right ear,
Like the Statue of Liberty ready to cast
Her lantern westward across the land,
And sighted me as I thudded the baked mud
Under our makeshift basket and wedged past
The last wispy evergreen on the right, one of five transplanted
From the woods to the no-man's land at our border.
I reached out to strum the leafless forsythia
At the far edge, more forsaken than any Ophelia-strung
Willow. I broke through into our estranged neighbor's
Double-plotted property, trespassed
Where his Presidential plums once stood,
Dipped under the clothesline, Mrs. Plant's pink
Panties still brushing the hair atop my head,
Passed Harvey's burnt-barrel incinerator,
And chugged on toward the virgin field
Up against the red picket fence
Guarding the Middlesex Village School.
Would I tumble at the drop-down edge,
Or get to the lush green grass in time,
Bomb and boy perfectly intersecting?
I looked up for the spiraling zeppelin,
White, with black rings at each end,
And found it, felt it, dropping hard,

Driving its point
Deep into the pit
Of my stomach,
Like an ICBM,
Just like.

Whom

I remember Tommy Bowden,

Who "stayed behind" two or three times,

Who was three years older than me,

Who was long-boned, hard-boned, man-size-boned

In boy-sized flesh,

Who haymakered my straw nose,

Flattening it even more;

Whose own hard-billed beak ran afoul

One raw fall day

All over the sleeves, front, and back of Peter Hildebrand,

Wrestling mate his own age,

Who himself turned out to be, or always was, gay;

Who (Tommy, that was)

Joined the Marines during the Vietnam War,

Or maybe it was the Special Services,

Or the Green Berets,

Or whatever,

Whom I lost track of,

Ultimately.

State

It's hard to think of another work whose interpretations so uncannily identify what the play calls the "form and pressure" of "the time." —James Shapiro

—So what's the big deal with Hamlet? said he.
—So many ghosts coming after, said I.
Thus, we thrusted, parried, and pared
In English 102, freshmen all.
—Hamlet is confused and constantly
   Has to talk to himself.
—Hamlet has to get his act together
   And take it on the road.
—Hamlet gets the point in the end,
   The point being,
   If he only had time to tell . . .

The point, perhaps,
An inspired sparrow
In insipient spiral?
But how came it silly-lily so?
Providence or Fat Fate?
Fat Hamlet letting be?
Readiness or ripeness all?
Then but now?

It's two unready sparrows I recall.

At 10,
From our back porch to the world,

Before the Kellys
And big brother Butch,
I was to BB
Through 40′ of courseless air,
Through still, unsparing leaves,
The unsuspecting sparrow.
It was a careless shot,
Followed by a careless fall,
Silly, really, an unexpected, plump
Plop.
But the stillness carried
And completed itself
In me.

Butch broke it as he would.
Having already boasted
Of pumping pigeons full of BBs,
He flinched not, set flight another 30′,
And fell from the neighbor's willow
His own sparrow.
It was brotherly love,
And the blackest of miracles.

Years passed, when,
In far distant and unrelated act,
Butch, lying at ready,
Flinched not with shotgun at 0′.
I cleaned blood and tissue,
Grains of marrow, grains of shell,

And found three shots in the midst.
I clutched them hard in warmth and sweat,
And kept them—

          Until one day,
Detecting some silliness in it all,
I pulled those teeth from my palm
And slung them back from our porch
Into the field beyond.
But nothing was to sow,
No Harryhausen skeleton warriors sprung up,
Just so many ghosts coming after.
—*At the end of the play,*
   Hamlet is in a state of death.

Raffle

Item: The Osteochondritis Dissecans Rag

Exercise, exorcise, or excise
Live evil, vile veil—I've l-
Iconned my entelechy to clastic syncopation:
    Oh, the hip bone's connected to the thigh bone,
        And the thigh bone's connected to the knee bone,
            And the knee bone's connected to being-been-bone.

I find myself, you see, numbered among the calamitous clan
Of hanky Hector, wounded knee by way of Achilles' heel,
    Hence cockatrice of a cicatrix, scar scare, serpent of my flesh
        Foul. Foul is, after all, fair, no squawking from your basic
            Basilisk, craven carved, chicken deboned. Of yore:
                Gordian knot hacked, gordian worm hatched.

So it is
      I'm do-did-done,
             being-been-bone,
                    and the number is—

Thirteen
      plus or minus
            pusillanimus.
                Yours to call.

The Case of the Mysterious Maiden

I imagine that Becky Covey did it,
With her figure a question mark,
In unmarked space,
Pointlessly

      Whirligig whirl-a-girl twirling about,
      How can you spin free from your self
      Spiritmint circles in the midday air?
      —However, the evidence is said not to exist.
      But in that case, what do I keep rump-a-bumping into,
      Why these subcircumstantial bruises,
      And wherefore this beguiling?

I suspect that Becky Covey did it,
With a Reggie reggae swoosh,
On the softball field,
Backwards.

      Pitch: whomp! . . . thump-ping, plop,
      Pitch: whomp! . . . thump-ping, plop,
      Female, white, brown hair, brown eyes, eleven years,
      Rips cover from rubberized,
      Balding, white male, age thirty-three.
      New screenball queen cops fresh means
      To uncle's end: "I love these nieces to pieces."

I pose that Becky Covey did it,
With a nonpoker presence,

In a cranberry cocktail pad on Cape Cod,
Wistfully.

> Passing fair to your fond
> Overbidding partner, you were unsuited
> To his unfolding: a lead mislaid
> And the game misplayed as the trumpeting
> Trickster was clubbed dumb, cut close,
> Dug deep, and, *au point*, disheartened.
> Your hard-earned hand lost,
> You conned a lingering sigh,
> Your breathlessness ensconcing
> In his forlorn conch forevermore.

I suggest that Becky Covey did it,
With anti-avocado anger,
Away from home,
Unapologetically.

> Bushwhacked by avuncular fruit and vegetable
> Riddles, puns, teases, and impatiences,
> You swung about and shot from the hip, only
> To get gunned down for good.
> Done for, felled from grace, you rose
> Up, burning brighter on the way out.
> Just so, avocado advocacy gave way
> To heart achoking.
> Let legumes be bygones.

That's it.
I accuse Becky Covey of doing away
With Mrs. White, Professor Plum, Mrs. Peacock,
Miss Scarlet, Mr. Green, Colonel Mustard,
Yours truly, and all and sundry she meets,
With a vivaciousness, indelicacy, and decidedness
All to her favor.
—But without a clue
How, how for, or how then.
A heart-stopper guilty of innocence,
To be sure.

Montlake, the Rest

A yellow leaf, midair-suspended, spinning-spinning by a thread,
Sets my eye, my mind, to turning, whirring,
Waiting the fall
Still to come.

Footprints in the frost, in shimmering, silvery frost,
Soon glide away,
Fade far away,
The imprint remaining on my mind, on the unforeseen dew.

Victorious geese,
Raucous wild geese,
Career across the wide, wildering sky, turning south,
Leaving youth, leaving me, leaving and returning me.

The sun coldly comes a-greeting, warming-to, soon chafing,
The red going out of the eastern sky, out of me,
As I look to
All the rest.

Blue

Beat the Devil

It all began with bogey man,
With rhythm bopping blues—Roll 'em!
A kinematic comptrolling
Of whirring, capital chaos,
Takes one to infinity—Cut!

Hump-free bump-free bogus artiste
Buggering bugbears with tough talk—
A stiff upper lip, a twitching cheek,
A mind fashioning lines to lisp
And sneer at bloody queens of hearts.

But spiritus fortis spluttered,
Flitting brows melted in mid-flight,
Virtu vesicated, scowls turned howls,
Winged lines fell to cancered chance,
The End—a spirant to mephistic bog art.

When

You left as a rag
Your red cotton flannel nightgown
With the white speckling flowers
Blue stamened

I was to tear the same
For wiping away the dust
From our old place
But not before one last play for time

Like the way my hands would search your sides
As they rolled away from me then back again
Both coming to rest
Where your soft belly slowly swelled

I never knew where one downy layer ended
And the other began
Or how they shifted and ran
And came to one

Like a woman now
A spirit in flight again
And then . . . and then . . .
I never knew when

Getting Along Swimmingly with a Male Friend

Behold the bones he called "impossible"—
Mistake, his part. Her ear? Rare cartilage,
Evidently quite real, a pink *coquille*
Brittle to blandishment, to male badinage
Of any sort, more so a would-be friend's.
He goes too far, along the jaw line yet,
Hermit crab drawing shell through softest sand,
White, waiting. No place for romance, she sets
Her chin. China, he'd have it, porcelain
Drawn up unbroken from Pacific depths
(So becomes their pool). She emerges green
Up under the dive, fish-boned, out of breath—
Behold calamity, all his the blame,
Raising the subliminal for the sublime.

That Tree

At the feet of the Lukachukai Mountains
There will always be a two-year-old
Singing pine cones back up onto
A living Christmas tree.
Off a way will be her father
Flat on the frozen earth
Sawing and sawing his way through
Until his tree falls
And his daughter sees
And cries for it.
He will bear that tree
Heavier than any before or since
Pricking jabbing blinding all the way
Until he too
Sees.

Colors

Frogs, she'd say, or maybe
It was squirrels, for Greeks,
If we drove past and
Their candles were all blue:
Their taste was all in their mouths.

We used orange, like many
Others in working class Lowell.
We were Americans, of
German and Lithuanian extraction.
That was back when some feature, ad,
Or riddle in a DC Green Lantern
Had me believe it snowed red in China.

Now, in the old frontier town of Squakheag,
Northfield, that is,
The genteel houses and immaculate
Churches are white, and so are their candles,
Except for the rectory at St. Patrick's, where
Father Jim uses green. Of course,
He drives a red Porsche, too.

Where does all this leave
Our family now, always late
And seeing the younger O'Briens below
Set forth white right after Thanksgiving?
What pressures, what decisions,
It's getting later still, something has to give . . .

Split the night already!
Go with red, green, orange, and blue
For each of us.
Plus white,
What the heck.

Waiting with Gatsby, *Syntactically*

Fitzgerald lives in his sentences, which is where writing lives, in sentences and human sympathy. —Adam Gopnik

Gatsby
    man of unknown past
        and very visible millions
waits
    at his mansion
    to see Daisy
    longing for his lost love
    his eyes staring across the bay
        at the starry green light
        at the end of Daisy's dock
with
    a roaring in his ears
    a rushing of his blood
us

On Michael Fung from Hong Kong

The so-called hard reality is that
Michael Fung has come to an end.
An end?
We are not finished with Michael,
And Michael is not finished with us,
And who knows if he or we ever will be.

Michael keeps popping up out of nowhere:
At midwinter term break in the claustrophobic youth hostel
Of Washington, D.C., ostensibly out of Georgetown,
There is Michael,
Those knowing, knowing eyes alone
Pushing back the walls.
Walls?

There he is, again, returned alum in the cramped,
Stuffy dorm lounge at prep school summer-vacating time
(How now out of Brown?),
Reaching out, warmly clasping with one hand,
The other, with perfect gentlemanliness, pulling down
The walls.
No walls for Michael.

Michael in a story about eating alone
In a Vietnamese restaurant, forgetting his wallet,
Being held captive in the kitchen,
Waiting for two hours for an aunt to come rescue him,
Leaving, saying, "I didn't say a word."

Michael's guidebook writing of "Different
Places at NMH": "Places to Study," "Places
To Socialize," and "Secret Places"—
"Actually, once the sky turns dark,
Every place at NMH can become
A secret place for anyone."

Michael's poem on eccentric friend
Adiyasa Dwitama of Indonesia
—*Being Adiyasa*—
As no other:
"*People always staring at me*
Because I am famous, handsome, and smart.
This is the reason why no one can replace
Me in the world.
Right on, Adi."

On Michael Fung from Hong Kong

Arbor Vitae

My hands, right over left, grip the five-foot
shaft chest-high, feel the hard-grained, finely grooved
wood, smooth as flesh stretched tender-taut. Then, yanking
the pole toward me while thrusting my hips skyward,
I rise to fall, to weight, to plunge the spade
head into giving, slitting, fertile earth.

My feet rest on blade's edge, straddling the pole's
base, my body suspended in space, poised,
standing on point to the blue-white sky—*Oh,*
get off it, keep going, you tooling fool, you.

So I back off, bend knees, shift hips, twist shoulders,
raising the spade head, breaking membranes, roots,
bearing off a moist, red-brown flow of dirt.
I shove and shovel, scoop and scope—I scop!—
singing out four-billion-year-old granite rocks,
and another blue-white pottery shard
left behind in this hard, Puritan-toiled
soil. So I am not the first. I would plant
arbor vitae. *Well, cerebellum, to it!*

Two-hour hole digging: six-feet long, three-feet
wide, fifteen-inches deep. Enough? Coyote-
proof? To mind: one last skyward leap, earthbound
plunge. To plain nowhere this time, metal clanking
on a boulder, shearing me off left. Yet
brought up short of an all-out sprawling fall,
banked by the (now) sun-dried, yellowing sand.

Remote Learning: The Talbot Test

Who doesn't fit:
Imhotep, Dracula, Frankenstein's monster,
Walking Dead guy, or dear old Larry Talbot?

How're they alike:
The flu, rubella, more measles, the mumps,
Polio, Covid-19, and Larry Talbot?

ID your LT match:
Depressed, repressed, regressed; first-, second-, third-
Shift; shapeshifting; plain shifty; all above.

Order by speed:
Sauropods, coronavirus mutation,
Film, light, LT hair growth, human constancy.

Reflect (short answer):
Sir T's *père-à-fils* parting help: "These people
Have a problem. You must make your own fight."

Brown

Last Leaves

She might have noticed how the brown oak leaves
Outlasted all the red maples, how oil
Made the difference, made the walkway connive

With the cold rain to cause her slip and fall.
There had to be cause to it, so far down,
How else explain the sudden jerk and pull of

Severed hand, down-pointed leaf in stiff run
Across ice-covered road, giving her start
To stop? Relieved over nothing, no one

Else to spare, she drove on, with little hurt
To life or illusion, only belief.
What to believe, standing behind pulled curtain,

When gust blew, out the window, selfsame leaf?
Some shock of recognition, sense of loss
Lingering? By March, no surprise, just love,

Seeing the leaf, on back, slide uphill (less
Snow, but just enough), back toward the oak shriven
Fast, but still unyielding of its last leaves.

It's okay, oak, really, they'll too be leaving;
She knows, better than ever, new life living.

Freckles

There seems to be some puzzling about
Just what freckles are offering up. Some hold
They're merely melanin, or brownish spots
On fair skin, with more pigmenting emboldened
By the sun—not even tanning, but sparks
Of the flesh, a flashing forth in response
To on-high, to stardust rekindled—quirks
That Hopkins in "Pied Beauty" saw and pondered
Over, science and poetry enmeshed
After all. So, glory be to the odd
Among the even, black on white, to wishes
And facts inseparable, to the id
Bio-, psycho-, other-logical, misses
Missed no more—human field of angels' kisses.

O

I will not grouse, not me, about the cold,
No ruffled feathers 'gainst the wind and snow.
Love the winter! It loves you back, we're told.
Behold my toes, see? They provide the show—
My feet grow pectens—yo, I go by snowshoes
Across the glaze! Good thing, because we hold
More weight, you know, the pounds packed on, no going
Easily about, layers in and out enfolded.
We compensate—eat more, heat more—so rosy
We grow, blaze even. Fast to come, I drove
Full speed last night, full heft, into the cozy
Snowdrift of our bed, white sheets, white wool—dove
Deeper still, snuggled in, a hole made home,
Whence to know, soft and warm, a pleasure dome.

Canticle

On the twelfth day of Christmas, or thereabouts,
My true love gave to me:
Some weird old man and weird old woman,
Some Simeon and an Anna—who would be heard,
Gracing us with these wild words about a sword
Through the soul, thoughts out of hearts,
Departing in peace, a stamp of redemption—
Anywho, thanks, all the same.

On the eleventh day of Christmas,
And the tenth and the ninth,
My true love gave to me:
. . . a whole lot of stuff.

On the eighth day of Christmas,
My true love gave to me:
A piece of skin, of all things,
White and bloody, but pure,
Circumspectly done, mind you, for
Flesh and blood are hardly palatable
As far as a taste in gifts goes;
"Priceless" in today's world, though, I guess.

On the seventh day of Christmas,
And the sixth and the fifth and the fourth,
My true love gave to me:
. . . a whole lot of stuff still.

On the third day of Christmas,
My true love gave to me:
Three golden rings,
Or maybe three golden kings,
Or some frankincense and myrrh
—Does anyone really know what those things are,
Today's aroma therapy?—
But golden stuff was in there, for sure.

On the second day of Christmas,
My true love gave to me:
Two turtledoves, or pigeons
(Although they only lasted to the twelfth),
Shepherds, animals, a Polish spider (go figure),
Bleating that went on and on and on,
Another kid whacking away at a drum—
It all made my head spin.

On the first day of Christmas,
My true love gave to me:
Well, True Love.
First and last.

Winter-Spring Swing

Hit it—
The little hill behind our house is popping, bopping—
It's bebopping!
It's bobbin'-robin time—
Black headed, black and white throated, gray coated, orange
Breasted, white bellied, yellow billed—you forage
Away, march about, dip, jerk, and flip them
Brown leafy clumps,
You here, you there,
You down and you up—it
Be everywhere,
Like a muddy hot spring
Bubbling at will, all aware—
Bird, Bud, Max, Miles, Curly, Tommy, Diz—bring in
Ella—you go, girl—you scat them boys—dare
'Em along—feed 'em, fun 'em, jazz 'em—
Muscling, moving, riffing, rolling spasm—
It ain't no algorithm!
No *algos*, man,
It *hedo*rhythm,
He *do* what she wants,
She *do* what he feels,
They *do* what pleases—
Hold it.

The Mourning Cloak

Nymphalis Antiopa

It's dark brown, mostly,
Thus seeming more moth than butterfly.
It doesn't die in winter
Or migrate to Mexico;
It hibernates in tree holes,
Or even under loose bark,
In cryo-preservation, possessing
Its own, natural anti-freeze
(One Hugh Newman once stored one
Successfully in his fridge, but failed
To raise and release the species in too-warm Britain).
It flies again by March,
Above any snowy ground,
And lights to bask in sunshine,
Absorbing solar heat, energy.
It sucks up nutrients, moisture, salts, and other minerals
From oak sap, rotted fruit, mud puddles, animal feces,
And human sweat.
It mates,
It dies,
The offspring emerge,
Mutate,
Estivate,
Re-emerge,
Then hibernate—

All told, the longest lived
Of all butterflies.
Its common name is puzzling,
Deriving, it appears, from some dark
Northern European, Nordic view—
Achtung, trauermantel!
Its uncommon name's the unsustainably
British "Camberwell Beauty"
Or "Grand Surprise."
Its scientific name is also puzzling,
The Zeus-as-satyr-seduced Antiope,
Long suffering of men,
Roaming mad on Kithairon,
Presumably by springs and streams,
So nymphal, riparian,
And saved of men,
And mother to twin sons.
So lay the stones,
As of the one son Zethos.

Across the Housatonic, up the trail
Toward Laura's Tower, past glacially strewn boulders,
We gaze at all the browns of March, the *feuille-*
Morte slope and barren hardwoods, a still coldness
Catching our breath, letting go.

                              Then, a deeper
And moving brown takes hold of us, a mourning
Cloak along our way, floating, gliding, sweeping

Down to bask among leaves earlier borne
To rest: oak, beech, hop hornbeam, maple, more.
We're pulled in close by the wings' whitish yellow,
Petticoat-peeping fringe—then band of stars,
Sapphires upon black velvet, as at Arles—
On into a rich cabernet brown, warming
Both the gazer and gazed upon.

                              But when
We get too close, she folds to cryptic form,
A charcoal-brown, striated, gray-lined ventral
Side, death-like—her camouflaging, surviving
Mode—ready to fly from danger, the sun,
And any mating urge. Indeed, she flies
Off, up the hill, toward the tower.

                              We continue
On, switchback with the rising path between
The sharper inclines, reach the crest, and stand
Before the stairs still left to climb . . . to see
What greater views above the trees we can
Achieve . . . to satisfy . . . Well, what? Who knows,
Some longing, leave it at that. The view does
Turn out fine: bigger sky, lakes, rivers, rows
Of rolling, evergreen-patched hills—but buzzing
Fear keeps flying at me. I must descend.

Ground gained, some glinting catches my eye: shards
Of broken beer bottles—brown, of course—when,

Why, what occasion or offering they served
We wonder briefly, let it go.

                   The mourning
Cloak swoops in, lands again close by, and calls
To us once more. This visit lasts much longer,

And we are first to leave this time, the hill
A gentle wending down, foot and wing, down.

So sing the stones of second son, Amphion.

The Two of You

I really do have two
Noses. Suppose you do, too.
All depends if you want to.

Care to give it a try?
Of course, you may ask why.
See, you've two hands, two eyes,

Two ears, even two minds
(Better than one?) at times,
And some say to be kind

You need to be cruel. Well,
Let's leave that aside. We'll
Deal first with physical

Things. Take your pointy, bossy
Index finger, make it cross
With the middle one, causing

A crevice you'll put ever
So gently on the tip of
Your nose. Wiggle right-left,

Left-right, back and forth—*presto!*
Two noses, no? Or yes,
That is? The bestest guess

How or why is the cells,
The nerves, send a signal
From each finger, so double

The feeling, meaning, for
Your mind! Is this important,
"Real"? A trick? Could be more.

I Sing the Body Molybdic

My love is like a green, green lima bean,
grainy yet buttery, fleshy yet fine,
glossy-smooth and tender-skinned,
both crescent-shaped and dimpled,
breasts to waist, hips to groin—

no dainty petal, fleeting scent, but protein-
filled, carb-rich *phaseolus lunatus*,
a sun-moon provenance
of vital elements,
of phosphorus and folate,

iron, manganese, and magnesium,
plus fiber, filtering my blood, my body—
this old eukaryote's
at last fully-fetched, risen,
O my molybdenum!

Withing

For Jane

Now, in once-winter, twilight figures rise up
across our oak-wise hill in fog and mist—
snow-conjured wraiths, gray-limbed, brown-cowled—
    and wisp
around the writhing, raw bittersweet, twists of
red-berried vines so thickened as to nestle
a wicker-child. What lies within, some post-
druidic, christian-extant sacrifice
to be? Of all Creation? Ash and dust
await, a matter of time it seems. Blood-
marked Christ, blood-dimmed tide? We must burn
    or drown,
at some point wake to know. Untouched, unmoved,
eternal second chances we would own.
What's befallen us, what's next to want and have,
are of no worth. Look to the always given.

Rodney Kleber is an educator, writer, actor, and director. His produced works include the ESL textbook *Build Your Case* (featuring sixteen Sherlock Holmes styled mysteries), plays, short fiction, and especially poetry. His comic verse drama *Coming to Light, An Advent Progress* premiered in December 2019 at the Northampton Center for the Arts. His poems have appeared in *Negative Capability, The Nation, Dappled Things, The Society of Classical Poets, The Ottawa Arts Review, The Deronda Review,* and *Slant.*